KITCHENER PUBLIC LIBRARY

W9-DGF-194
-2

# Persuasion Equation
## The Subtle Science of Getting Your Way

**MARK RODGERS**

**AMACOM**
**AMERICAN MANAGEMENT ASSOCIATION**
New York • Atlanta • Brussels • Chicago • Mexico City • San Francisco
Shanghai • Tokyo • Toronto • Washington, D.C.

Bulk discounts available. For details visit:
www.amacombooks.org/go/specialsales
Or contact special sales:
Phone: 800-250-5308
E-mail: specialsls@amanet.org
View all the AMACOM titles at: www.amacombooks.org
American Management Association: www.amanet.org

This publication is designed to provide accurate and authoritative information in regard to the subject matter covered. It is sold with the understanding that the publisher is not engaged in rendering legal, accounting, or other professional service. If legal advice or other expert assistance is required, the services of a competent professional person should be sought.

**Library of Congress Cataloging-in-Publication Data**
Rodgers, Mark, 1965-
    Persuasion equation : the subtle science of getting your way / Mark Rodgers.
        pages cm
    Includes bibliographical references and index.
    ISBN 978-0-8144-3417-8 (pbk. : alk. paper) — ISBN 0-8144-3417-7 (pbk. : alk. paper) —
    ISBN 978-0-8144-3418-5 (e-book : alk. paper)  1. Negotiation in business.  2. Persuasion
(Psychology)  3. Success in business.  4. Decision making.  I. Title.
    BF637.P4R53 2015
    303.3'42--dc23                                                                    2014042351

© 2015 Mark Rodgers.
All rights reserved.
Printed in the United States of America.

This publication may not be reproduced, stored in a retrieval system, or transmitted in whole or in part, in any form or by any means, electronic, mechanical, photocopying, recording, or otherwise, without the prior written permission of AMACOM, a division of American Management Association, 1601 Broadway, New York, NY 10019.

The scanning, uploading, or distribution of this book via the Internet or any other means without the express permission of the publisher is illegal and punishable by law. Please purchase only authorized electronic editions of this work and do not participate in or encourage piracy of copyrighted materials, electronically or otherwise. Your support of the author's rights is appreciated.

**About AMA**
American Management Association (www.amanet.org) is a world leader in talent development, advancing the skills of individuals to drive business success. Our mission is to support the goals of individuals and organizations through a complete range of products and services, including classroom and virtual seminars, webcasts, webinars, podcasts, conferences, corporate and government solutions, business books, and research. AMA's approach to improving performance combines experiential learning—learning through doing—with opportunities for ongoing professional growth at every step of one's career journey.

Printing number

10  9  8  7  6  5  4  3  2  1

To my precious wife, Amy;
all things are possible because of you.

# CONTENTS

I vividly remember a phone call in 1985, when a woman I didn't know asked if I was Alan Weiss.

"Yes, I am," I said.

"And do you own a Mercedes 450 SLC?" she asked.

"Yes, I do," I admitted, expecting perhaps a factory recall advisory.

"Well, how would you like to own one of the very first car phones in New England?" she prompted.

"I'm free this afternoon," I said, and I acquired a hard-wired handset, which was the first of the phones in every car I subsequently owned until the advent of cell phones.

I remember this so clearly because it was the last "cold call" purchase I ever made, and because it was so elegantly simple. Today, we'd call that series of questions and answers "consistency," since it relies on a continuing affirmative response. I simply called it "Wow!"

Persuasion takes many forms, but the underlying principles are clear: We should seek commitment, not merely compliance; speed is highly desirable (the longer you wait, the more bad things happen); and finding others' self-interests and adapting to them is essential.

Mark Rodgers is the expert in persuasive powers. He is a veteran consultant, working with major corporations. He's a previously published author. And he's a superb coach. In this book, he's distilled the key techniques to galvanize others and marshal their support. You'll learn in the pages that follow that there's a momentum in passion that can be maneuvered in your favor, just as an expert in martial arts can move a larger opponent using the other's momentum.

Too many managers believe that they are trying to convince when they are actually trying to coerce. They seek to influence behaviors rather than change beliefs. Their thinking is self-centered rather than other-centered. Hierarchical power can command but not necessarily persuade. These are subtle but powerful distinctions, which the reader can ignore only at great peril.

We see the lessons every day. A president and Congress at an impasse, with no one seemingly able to reach a compromise. Yet we know it's possible within either party, since both Ronald Reagan and Bill Clinton were superb at finding the grounds to enact legislation with bipartisan support. We seem to live in a polarized world, where there are "social media" but not "business media," and people are encouraged to take sides and take up causes rather than take an open view and find the means to make things work. The "social" aspect of social media seems to be entirely false.

How important is persuasion amid these trends? I've been consulting for 30 years and visited 60 countries, and I've never seen an organization with unhappy employees and happy customers. I've never failed to see unhappy customers persuade others *not* to patronize their object of dislike. Yet, I've often stood at Fifth Avenue and 60th Street in New York City to watch 1,000 people line up to get the very first of a new line of Apple products, which they could get at their leisure if they just waited a month. (And I've marveled at the Apple employees who emerge before the store opens to offer the crowd juice and snacks.)

Every day we are required to influence, recommend, cajole, nudge, suggest, advise, and threaten. We engage in these activities proactively to build consensus and support. We throw ourselves in reactively, because we've been wronged or tricked or had a march stolen on us. Politics, advertising, entertainment, health care—you name it, they rely on persuasion. Smoking has been reduced substantially, because the public has been persuaded both through education and appeals to personal needs (such as living to enjoy your grandchildren and not killing family members through secondhand smoke).

Persuasion can be macro or micro. The techniques and approaches Mark provides are brilliant because they are pragmatically useful every day. They can be used with coworkers or family members, in civic meetings or service settings. They are ubiquitous and powerful, yet stunningly simple to apply.

I invite you to enjoy the journey ahead, hoping that I've whet your appetite and persuaded you to pay close attention. I can't imagine the day when I wouldn't want to have a phone in my car, and I still thank that wonderful saleswoman who knew how to help me. Read on, and allow Mark to help you.

—**Alan Weiss, Ph.D.**, author of 55 books, including
*Million Dollar Consulting* and *Thrive!*

## ACKNOWLEDGMENTS

I'd like to thank Bob Nirkind, the terrifically talented senior acquisitions editor at AMACOM. His support, dedication, and guidance made this project a reality. It was also Bob's excellent judgment that added Alison Hagge to this project. She's an enormously gifted editor, who carefully thought through every detail, making this business book read like a novel. I'd also like to thank my literary agent, John Willig, who is also an advocate and friend; he is simply one of the best in the business.

Just when I thought I'd heard it all in my career, I found Alan Weiss. Alan has been a mentor, coach, confidant, and guide to me for almost a decade. He's left an indelible impression on me, and you'll see his influences all over my work. I'd also like to acknowledge the late Joel DeLuca, another terrific mind, who was very important to my development.

It's difficult to express just how critical my draft editor, Michael Popke, has been to this project. He and I have faced down more deadlines than I care to remember, and he is the reason we succeed. Michael Popke is as good as they come.

I'd also like to thank those who contributed to the book. This list no doubt will not be all-inclusive and is in no particular order: Julie Terberg, Bob Bell, Bruno Shirripa, Daniel Stern, Eric Dorobiala, Marc Eisenhower, Billy Friess, Gary Ramey, Jody Gunderman, Pat Inks, Jenne Meyer, Lara Lee, Sally Strackbein, Roberta Matuson, Richard Citrin, Hugh Blaine, Judy Chan, Daniel Lock, Leslie Prevish, Kathy Koshgarian, and Kathy Morris.

I'd like to thank our small, but close-knit, family, whose support we treasure. And finally, my most important thank-you goes to my wife, Amy, who makes all things possible.

## INTRODUCTION

"If you were being banished to a desert island and could take only one record with you, what album would you take?"

I've always been fascinated by this question, for two reasons. First, what legal system is handing down island banishments, and how do I get convicted? Second, they still have record players?!

Oddly enough, that's the question that sparked my idea for this book. After pondering that dilemma, I asked myself, "If someone were to have room on their bookshelf (or space on their Kindle) for just one business book on persuasion, what book would it be?"

I've spent almost three decades helping people hear yes more often, and I've finally decided to put in one place everything you need to go from zero to persuasion hero. This book will not sway opinions about global warming, bring peace to the Middle East, or abolish man's inhumanity to man. But it *will* help you.

The world of big business abounds with major persuasion plays. Time Warner Cable wants you to switch from DirecTV. Dunkin' Donuts wants you to abandon Starbucks. But you want your coworkers to get on board with your idea, and that's our focus here. (One of the most frequent questions I'm asked: "Will this stuff work on my kids?" It sure will! But use it at the office first, so you can afford college.)

### PERSUASION CHALLENGES

The ideas presented here will enable you to get that plum assignment, receive the green light on that project, and vie successfully for your dream job. Along the way, this book will help you solve professional challenges such as:

1. Who do you want to persuade to do what?

2. Are your persuasion objectives ethical?

3. How should you approach your target?

4. When should you make your persuasive move?

5. How do you know if you can trust someone?

6. How can you win someone's trust?

7. How can you make your arguments more compelling?

8. What specifically should you say?

9. How can you recover from a setback?

10. How can you best leverage success?

11. How do you create perpetual yes?

If the science of persuasion were paint by numbers, everyone would be Picasso. It isn't, and they aren't. That's why this book is your competitive advantage. What follows on the pages to come are tools to help you master the art of persuasion.

## PERSUASION SOLUTIONS

In Chapter 1, "Persuasion Fundamentals," you'll discover the Persuasion Paradox, and learn if you truly are "made to persuade." You'll develop a specific persuasion priority and set your sights on dramatic career improvement. I'll also reveal the ultimate persuasion principle.

In Chapter 2, "Decision Making," I'll introduce you to the world of heuristics and cognitive biases, showing you how people's brains are wired and how you can use that information to ethically pursue yes. Next, in Chapter 3, "Targets, Technology, and Tactics," I'll uncover the persuasion keys to working with different personality types, gender gaps, and generational differences. I'll also address the changing nature of computer-mediated communication and include a discussion about how you can identify the fine line between ethical persuasion and manipulation.

Chapters 4 through 7 include what I call the "Persuasion Equation." This is the combination of factors will add up to your success:

(A Great Business Case  +  Your Outstanding Credibility  + Compelling Language)  ×  Intelligent Process  =  Yes Success

In these chapters, I'll teach you how to run the numbers by calculating your Return on Investment (even if you're terrified of a calculator), as well as show you how to leverage emotion and measure the unmeasurable. I'll help you build your credibility, explain how to win it back when you lose it, and divulge the power of language and the language of power. You'll learn to weave a tale, tickle a funny bone, and do it all in a way that creates your personal inimitable marketplace superiority. You'll unwrap a powerful persuasion process that, like following stepping-stones across a stream, will easily lead you to yes. (Learning persuasion skills is so essential to business success that I've created a special *Persuasion Equation* section on our website, www.PersuasionMatters.com, that will take you beyond the information in this book.)

Once you've conquered the world of one-on-one persuasion, Chapter 8, "Persuasion 360," will show you how to generate group buy-in and navigate the contentious challenges of organizational politics with a terrific tool called "Political Territory Mapping." In Chapter 9, "Persuasion 911," I'll introduce you to "assent turbulence" and describe emergency actions you can take to pilot your way to a safe landing. In Chapter 10, "Yes Success," I'll show you how to respond in that thrilling moment of yes, as well as explain why most people respond to yes incorrectly. You'll also learn how to leverage testimonials and referrals, while creating personal evangelists to help you achieve perpetual yes.

In Chapter 11, "Your Persuasion Action Plan," I'll introduce a step-by-step plan to help you realize a 10,000-to-1 return on your investment in this book. (Yes, it's exciting stuff—and I guarantee results if you apply the ideas. If you don't, all bets are off.) In the final chapter, "The

Psychology of Self-Persuasion," I'll help you build weapons-grade self-esteem, self-efficacy, and self-confidence, leading to an ever-expanding universe of yes. I call it "Mark's Psychological Big Bang," because the first person who needs to say yes is . . . *you*.

## PERSUASION CAVEAT

Persuasion is not magic. It doesn't cure every ill or solve every problem. People constantly say to me, "Well, you're an expert on persuasion, so just persuade them." Unfortunately, it's rarely that simple.

If you practice the ideas in this book, you *will* hear yes more often. But persuasion won't work every time. If an opposing economic argument is too overpowering, few things will alter that course. However, if you're close in terms of economic benefit to both parties, the approaches in this book can tip the scales in your favor. In a world where cash is king, persuasion is your ace.

## *THE PERSUASION EQUATION*

When people ask me what album I would take if banished to a desert island, my response comes easily: I would choose the self-titled second album from The Band—a masterpiece from a musical group that used the definite article because its members knew they were the definite article.

So is this book. If you have space on your shelf for only a single book about persuasion, let *this* be the one.

# Persuasion Fundamentals

**The Basics You Need to Know, and
Why You Need to Know Them**

*"Will you do it?"*

The surrounding offices were still and dark. Even the up-and-comers had gone home for the evening. An ancient vacuum's tortured whine pierced the quiet as the nighttime custodial crew worked its way down the hall. The hum of the cheap fluorescent lights overhead added an interrogation-room quality to the discussion.

Sally Matheson, the marketing vice president in charge of the project, waited patiently, her calmness masking the fact that a multimillion-dollar project's deadline hung on the answer to the question she'd asked just minutes ago. IT Vice President Peter Simmons—the best in the organization, maybe the business—had heard Sally ask for help countless times during the past five years; he knew her well.

Sally faced one of the toughest persuasion challenges: peer to peer. She had no ability to reward or punish. No desire to threaten or cajole. Everything boiled down to this relationship and her ability to persuade.

\* \* \*

Has your success ever hinged on someone agreeing with your initiative? Have you ever watched a project fail due to lack of buy-in? Stood dumbfounded as someone else was handed the promotion you coveted? Watched a potential client pass on your proposal in favor of a more charismatic competitor?

Whether you are in the executive suite, in middle management, or on the front lines, persuasion skills are crucial to ensuring that you have the best chance of career success. If you internalize the concepts in this book, you will be able to ethically convince more people to get on board with your ideas, more quickly and more effectively than you ever imagined. You'll be able to generate organizational "buzz" for your initiatives, your results, and you, creating professional evangelists who will sing your praises.

In meeting rooms, hall chats, and off-site gatherings, the word will be: "You can't move on that project until you talk to her." Or "Don't even try to launch that product without consulting him." Not because you hold some hierarchical power or budget (although that may be the case), but rather because you have such professional gravitas.

In order to reach that point in your workplace environment, though, you need to start somewhere. Let's begin with key definitions.

## WHAT IS PERSUASION?

To the uninitiated, the term *persuasion* has negative connotations. "You're not going to persuade me!" they say defiantly. Or the well-intentioned person may proclaim, "I would never try to *persuade* someone."

Persuasion is not coercive, conniving, or devious. Drop that inaccurate psychological baggage right now. No one can be persuaded to do something he or she doesn't want to do. The person may have second thoughts or buyer's remorse, but that's another subject entirely.

I define *persuasion* as "ethically winning the heart and mind of your target." Let's take a moment to examine this definition word by word. *Ethically* means simply doing something honestly and without trickery or deceit. *Winning* means gaining agreement with your suggestion, idea, or position. *Heart* refers to gaining emotional buy-in, *mind* refers to logical buy-in, and *target* represents the specific person you are attempting to persuade. (To make the ideas presented here more accessible, the first seven chapters will look at persuasion through a one-on-one lens; Chapter 8 will cover how to apply persuasion in group settings.)

A term often used in conjunction with persuasion is *influence*. Influence is the capacity to become a compelling force that produces effects on the opinions, actions, and behavior of others. Occasionally, I'll use the term influence as an effect that "nudges" a target toward thinking positively about my request. But I'd like for you to primarily think of influence as your professional and personal credibility, your organizational and political capital, your corporate "sway." Persuasion is an action; influence is a state or condition.

I'll say this again: One thing persuasion is *not*? Manipulation. Nor is it underhanded or self-serving. Could you use the tactics in this book in a manipulative and self-serving manner? Sure. Will you reach agreement? Absolutely!

Once.

After that, your persuasive powers with that particular person will be all but finished. Manipulation does not help build long and lucrative careers. Whether you're attempting to persuade or dissuade, you have to be doing it for the right reasons and in the right manner. Here and there, I'll point out how some people use persuasive tactics in ways that are clearly manipulative (such as the real "Wolf of Wall Street"), while some companies and brands skate the fine line between ethical and manipulative persuasion. However, my underlying assumption, as author, is that you, as reader, will always be operating with the best interests of your target, your clients, and your organization in mind.

## TWO PRIMARY ROLES OF PERSUASION

To understand what persuasion can do for you and your career, we must begin by clarifying the two fundamental roles of persuasion. The first involves getting someone to say yes to your offer or request—to buy your product, agree to your idea, or take you up on your suggestion. Persuasion helps you get someone to willingly *do* something. You may want that person to:

- *Approve a higher head count:* "Will you sign off on my four new field sales positions?"

- *Enter into a business relationship:* "Do we have a deal?"

- *Support your initiative:* "Will you back my proposal at the board meeting?"

The second role of persuasion—and one that many people over-look—is getting someone *not* to do something, to *dissuade* him or her from taking action you feel might be harmful, such as using a particular supplier or launching a particular product. For example, you may want that person to:

- *Not go ahead with a new business partnership:* "That firm is just bouncing back from bankruptcy; do you think we should partner with it?"

- *Discontinue, or at least rethink, an existing initiative:* "Our East Coast teams aren't seeing much client interest."

- *Change a decision, or at least continue due diligence:* "Do you think he is the right person for the job? If we keep looking, we might be able to find a better fit."

Law enforcement officers in San Francisco use the power of dis-suasion very effectively. Bicycle thefts are so widespread that a special task force uses GPS-tagged bait bikes to catch would-be thieves, which forces small-time criminals to ask themselves one significant question before they steal: Is this a bait bike?

If you're going to thrive in the eat-or-be-eaten contemporary work-place, you must be able to effectively use both roles. This book provides you with a competitive advantage, because your competitors are more than likely not focusing on their own persuasion skills. Why? Consider a condition I call the "Persuasion Paradox."

## THE PERSUASION PARADOX

In a nutshell the Persuasion Paradox can be summarized thus: Although persuasion is crucial to people's success for many reasons, they actually spend very little time and effort improving their persuasion skills. In fact, at best, many professionals take a mindless approach to persuasion. At worst, they abhor the practice of persuasion, striving to avoid it. The mindless ones, either consciously or subconsciously, assume that just because they've heard people say yes to them—and they've given the same response to others—they understand the complexities of attaining agreement. This supposition couldn't be further from the truth. The act of persuasion remains a significant obstacle for many professionals, and they might not even be aware of it. However, like failing to check your blind spot before darting out into the oncoming lane on a narrow highway to pass a slow-moving vehicle, ignoring this obstacle can lead to disastrous results.

The ones who abhor persuasion treat it like a dead rodent. They want nothing to do with it, think it smacks of the dreaded word *sales* and conjures images of white shoes, plaid jackets, and glad-handing used-car salesmen. But successful people, who are neither mindless nor abhorrent, don't see persuasion that way. Professionals at the top of their game understand not only that it is okay for them to promote their ideas and issues, but that it is incumbent on them to do so.

Having someone say yes to your ideas, offers, and suggestions ranks among the greatest achievements in the business world. It represents validation, respect, and acceptance among your peers and others. In author Daniel Pink's survey of American workers, "What Do You Do at Work?" for his book, *To Sell Is Human: The Surprising Truth About Moving Others* (New York: Riverhead Books, 2012), he discovered full-time, non-sales workers spent 24 out of every 60 minutes involved in persuasion efforts. To say effective persuasion is merely important is to make an extreme understatement.

Persuasion requires intellectual heavy lifting. Understanding your target, knowing how to increase the value of your offering (or, conversely, decrease the resistance of your target), choosing the right words, and determining the timing of your persuasive efforts all are prerequisites of effective persuasion. The fact that you are reading this book means you're willing to take steps to break out of the Persuasion Paradox. No approach or technique can guarantee persuasion success, but if you put into practice the ideas and advice found on these pages, you will dramatically increase your chances.

So, let's talk about *you* and yes.

## SETTING YOUR PERSUASION PRIORITY

Let's consider your career. If, in your professional endeavors, you could flick a switch and convince one person to do just one thing, what would that be? Do you want to get the assignment? Bring a new product to market? Overhaul the Customer Service Department? Win the promotion? Land a big-name client? Secure a budget increase?

Each of these is what I call a "persuasion priority." To get to the heart of the matter, ask yourself this: *Who* is the one person you want to say yes, and to *what*? Note: When setting persuasion priorities, it's often more effective to state them in the affirmative, even if you're attempting to dissuade someone. For example, if you want your target to *not* choose a particular vendor, phrase your priority along these lines: "I would like Steve to weigh other options before choosing his vendor." Before you answer the above persuasion priority question, consider the four persuasion priority criteria. Your persuasion priority must be:

1. *Meaningful:* Important to you and your organization

2. *Significant:* Large enough to make a difference in your life and workplace

3. *Realistic:* But not so large a request that it's unattainable

4. *Others-Oriented:* Because you get ahead by improving the condition of others

Be specific, too. Avoid generalizing with a statement such as, "I'd like my boss to give me more responsibility." That's too imprecise. To increase your chances of persuasion success, specificity is crucial: "I want my boss to give me responsibility for the Latin American project." Don't say: "I want my senior vice president to add some people to my staff." Instead, say: "I want my senior vice president to approve five key new hires for my department next quarter."

Stop reading right now and write down your persuasion priority, which you will keep in mind as you work your way through this book:

I want _____ to _____

_____

_____.

Of course, at any given time, you'll have multiple issues and objectives for which you seek agreement. But if you'd like to receive the biggest return on your investment of time and money in this book, keep your persuasion priority top of mind. As you move through these pages, strategies and approaches will emerge to significantly increase your chances of getting to yes. And if you've chosen your objective carefully, achieving it will have a dramatic and overwhelmingly positive impact on your career—and perhaps your life.

## SELF-TEST: ARE YOU MADE TO PERSUADE?

Behavior is how you conduct yourself in a given situation. In professional settings, wildly persuasive people balance the following attributes:

- *Assertive:* Inclined to be bold and self-assured

- *Empathetic:* Possess the ability to see the world from another person's perspective

- *Communicative:* Adept at applying verbal and nonverbal communication

- *Tenacious:* Extremely persistent when adhering to or accomplishing something

- *Resilient:* Possess the ability to recover quickly after hearing no

## Evaluating Your Skill Sets

Now it is time for you to evaluate your natural persuasive abilities. Rank yourself in each of the five areas based on the descriptions above. A word to the wise: Doing "well" on this self-test isn't about scoring 10 in each area; it's about possessing the right blend of these key behaviors. After all, a strength overdone is a weakness. (Let's say you have great voice inflection and people find you an engaging and persuasive public speaker. Go too far with that voice inflection, though, and you'll sound like a crazy—and not-at-all-convincing—late-night infomercial host.)

So be honest in your self-critique. And try to resist the temptation to peek at the scoring while you're doing this. This self-test will be most useful to you if you have honest results.

### Assertive

*Low:* You rarely ever raise a new or contentious issue with others.

*Medium:* You regularly speak out in meetings and present cases for your statements.

*High:* Others might describe you as hardheaded or strongly opinionated.

| Low | | | | Medium | | | | | High |
|-----|---|---|---|--------|---|---|---|---|------|
| 1 | 2 | 3 | 4 | 5 | 6 | 7 | 8 | 9 | 10 |

## Empathetic

*Low:* You rarely consider another person's perspective.

*Medium:* You easily determine when others want or don't want to continue a conversation.

*High:* You've cried tears of joy at another's success.

| Low | | | | Medium | | | | High | |
| --- | --- | --- | --- | --- | --- | --- | --- | --- | --- |
| 1 | 2 | 3 | 4 | 5 | 6 | 7 | 8 | 9 | 10 |

## Communicative

*Low:* You tell everyone the same thing, the same way; you also send a lot of group emails.

*Medium:* You can explain most things to most people.

*High:* You intentionally vary both verbal and nonverbal approaches to suit your audience.

| Low | | | | Medium | | | | High | |
| --- | --- | --- | --- | --- | --- | --- | --- | --- | --- |
| 1 | 2 | 3 | 4 | 5 | 6 | 7 | 8 | 9 | 10 |

## Tenacious

*Low:* You try to convince people of an idea, but you're not going to force them to agree with you.

*Medium:* When you want something, you'll keep trying to get it for a good long time.

*High:* You hold on to your positions and objectives forever.

| Low | | | | Medium | | | | High | |
| --- | --- | --- | --- | --- | --- | --- | --- | --- | --- |
| 1 | 2 | 3 | 4 | 5 | 6 | 7 | 8 | 9 | 10 |

## Resilient

*Low:* When people say no to you, you feel personally rejected and depressed for days or weeks.

*Medium:* When rejected, you feel down, reflect on what happened, then move on.

*High:* Nobody likes to hear no, but you quickly shrug it off and move forward.

| Low | | | | Medium | | | | | High |
|---|---|---|---|---|---|---|---|---|---|
| 1 | 2 | 3 | 4 | 5 | 6 | 7 | 8 | 9 | 10 |

## Interpreting Your Results

Here's my take on the optimum score for each essential behavior:

*Assertive:* Ideally, you should score around a 7 here. You certainly can't be devoid of assertiveness and be considered persuasive; at the same time, if you gave yourself a 10, you might have already crossed the line from assertive to aggressive.

*Empathetic:* An 8 is great. You can't be tone-deaf to the other person's needs, but you also shouldn't make your objectives completely subservient to your target's every whim. You want to put yourself in the other person's shoes temporarily—not live there.

*Communicative:* This is where you want to hit the persuasive ball out of the park. Communication skills are crucial. What you say, how you say it, where you say it, when you say it, and what you're wearing all count. You want to be at your best, using both verbal and nonverbal communication to suit the message needs of your audience in much the same way a chameleon changes colors depending on mood and circumstances.

*Tenacious:* This one might surprise you. To be a persuasive professional, you should score only about a 5 or 6 on the tenacity scale. If you hold on to your ideas too tightly, you may quickly establish the reputation of someone who is unreasonable or obstinate. The key to knowing when you've gone too far is having the ability to decode corporate-speak. When people start telling you they "like your passion," that's code for "We think you've lost your mind." When you hear that, ease off the throttle.

*Resilient:* You need to score around a 9 here, because you will face a lot of rejection in your career. No one hears yes all the time, so you better learn how to handle no appropriately. If someone doesn't like your suggestion for the new marketing campaign, and you sulk about it for weeks, considering it as some sort of personal condemnation, you're setting yourself up for a brutal existence. I'm not suggesting that you be completely unfazed by rejection, however; momentary unhappiness can stimulate you to reflect and make important and necessary adjustments. But the key here is taking action after hearing no. Do you get back to work quickly? People who score a 9 in resiliency do.

It's important to understand that your ability to improve is not based on some sort of inherent genetic disposition. You don't need to be born with a silver tongue in order to be successful at persuasion. If you naturally have what it takes to be a persuasive individual, congratulations! The following chapters will amplify those strengths. But if you aren't a natural, find reassurance in the fact that persuasion skills can be acquired, and know that the information here will dramatically improve your persuasive abilities.

## PERSUASION PRECEPTS

Now that we've defined persuasion and its purposes, explored your immediate persuasion priority, and examined behaviors necessary for persuasion success, let's turn our attention to three key foundational ideas on which your persuasive efforts will be built. These ideas are reciprocity (the linchpin of persuasion), a fascinating concept referred to as "enlightened self-interest," and the ultimate persuasion principle: congruency.

### Reciprocity
Reciprocity is a fundamental human condition that means a "cooperative interchange," or the repaying of others in kind, often for a mutually beneficial result. This give-and-take understanding between humans is essential to our existence—it's basically the reason our species has endured on this planet. Reciprocity is about surviving—and thriving—

within your own organization. Likewise, understanding reciprocity is vital to maximizing your yes success.

And the first step to doing so involves establishing a healthy give-and-take mindset. The matrix in Figure 1-1 will help you think about how you currently leverage (or don't leverage) reciprocity. There are two planes to consider: your willingness to actively do things for others, and your willingness to accept assistance from others.

Do you "give" a lot? Do you provide favors, information, and insight to others? Or do you keep to yourself? Do you willingly accept favors, information, and insight? Or do you insist on going it alone, like a solo climb up Mount Everest? Let's evaluate each mindset.

**Martyr.** If you give a lot but accept very little in return, you're creating a martyr-like professional condition. In his purest form, a martyr either suffers greatly or is willing to die for his cause. Sometimes, professionals give without receiving, but they don't for long, because it's simply not a sustainable position. One reason people find themselves playing the role of martyr is because they refuse to accept reciprocated behavior. How many times have you heard yourself saying this to a colleague trying to return a favor: "No, that's all right—no need to repay me." Granted, you might say that in an effort to be magnanimous. But don't. In a situation where the other person's perceived obligation to repay you is strong, she may actually *like you less* if you don't allow her to reciprocate. Drop the martyr act.

**Modest.** By failing to help others—and likewise failing to accept others' help—you're allowing no one to benefit from your presence. That greatly diminishes your contribution to others and your organization. This type of behavior may very well have provoked Oliver Wendell Holmes to write: "Alas for those that never sing, But die with all their music in them!" If you don't give or take, you'll always be stuck in neutral.

**Machiavellian.** Niccolò Machiavelli's portrait in world history has been painted with a black brush, largely because of the Italian politi-

**Figure 1-1** Give-and-Take Mindsets

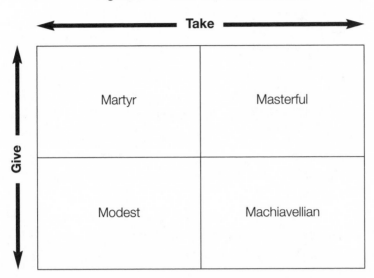

cian's views on winning, losing, and manipulation. You might be similarly casting a shadow on your reputation if you operate in a manner that others perceive as selfish. You succeed when you create allies, not adversaries.

Does someone in your organization constantly ask for favors but not even attempt to repay them? Does that person always seem to take credit for the work of others? Does he or she promise the world but never deliver even a small corner of it? You bet. Pause now and take note of the negative feelings you're experiencing by merely *thinking* about people like that and their actions. That's because they offend your sense of justice. Make sure you're not acting in a Machiavellian manner; otherwise, people will be thinking of you with that same outrage.

**Masterful.** When you give generously and accept repayment in kind, you both contribute greatly and benefit greatly. Best of all, people will think highly of you. The "Masterful" quadrant is where you want to spend most of your time. One of the main reasons people don't find themselves in this quadrant nearly enough is that they fear their contributions will not be reciprocated. Don't get caught thinking that way. Not to go all "California woo-woo" on you, but if you do good things, good things will happen to you. (Later, I'll show you how to nudge karma in your direction.)

Helping someone by reviewing his presentation, or obtaining a piece of information a coworker needs, or serving as a sounding board while a colleague from another department vents all rank as valuable behaviors you can provide for others. When you do these—or implement any similar positive reciprocity behavior—your actions likely will be reciprocated. This is the necessary give-and-take nature of the persuasively masterful.

Do not misinterpret the give-and-take mindset as tit for tat. This is a general guiding notion, not an accounting ledger. You want to help others and accept their reciprocal actions, not track how many minutes you've given and then expect the same in return. (Do that and people will call you other names!)

### How Senses Affect Persuasion Efforts

The type of beverage you drink, the surface of the chair on which you sit, and the color of clothing you wear all play a role in getting to yes (or no) faster. Thalma Lobel, a Ph.D. and director of the Child Development Center at Tel Aviv University, maintains that decisions, judgments, and values are derived as much from outside factors as they are from our brains. In her 2014 book, *Sensation: The New Science of Physical Intelligence* (New York: Atria Books), Lobel provides scientific evidence of how targets respond to common situations that, on the surface, appear insignificant:

- People drinking warm beverages such as coffee or tea are judged by their targets to be more generous, caring, and good-natured than those enjoying such cold beverages as soda or iced coffee. The concept of "warm" and "cold" extends beyond the drink and transfers to the individual drinking it.

- That "warm/cold" mentality is at play in other facets of our lives, too. Take the chair you opt to sit in while making your pitch. Studies suggest harder chairs make people tougher negotiators, while softer chairs reduce their aggressiveness. Hmmm. Maybe you should add a soft and comfy chair to your office for guests . . .

- Researchers found that men consider women who wear a red blouse (as opposed to a blue, green, or gray blouse) consistently more attractive. Red represents strength, power, and energy. Wear it when you need to hear yes.

**Enlightened Self-Interest (and Other Persuasive Methods)**

Although technology, society, demographics, and economies have changed greatly as the world has evolved, some persuasive patterns remain remarkably unaltered. The oldest method of getting someone to do something is through a reward-or-punish approach, typically known as using a "carrot" or a "stick." Common business incentives include an increase in compensation, recognition, or responsibility. That's the "carrot" side of this equation; the "stick" side involves punishing someone for either doing or not doing something. (Pay is docked, participation in a project is canceled, or the highly anticipated business trip is withheld.) Rewards and punishments are largely considered coercive actions. The moment you remove the coercion (the carrot or the stick), the coerced individual regresses to previous behavior. Long-lasting career success requires real agreement, not a momentary nod.

Another age-old approach to attaining buy-in is through normative means, or via the "social norms" of a group—as in, all the kids are doing it. This is a difficult way to reliably achieve agreement because people are so mercurial. Today, you must be savvier than ever in your approaches to persuasiveness. And the savviest approach of all involves appealing to your target's enlightened self-interest.

The concept of enlightened self-interest is largely attributed to the 19th-century French historian and social observer Alexis de Tocqueville and his landmark work, *Democracy in America*. De Tocqueville's idea involves doing things that are positive and right (profitable and ethical, in other words). If it's positive for you (your increased income, your heightened professional status, your strengthened organization), positive for other parties involved (your target and your target's organization), and positive for the larger whole in which you operate (your industry or your community), then why not do it? Self-interest can be good; enlightened self-interest can be tremendous. Appeal to the enlightened self-interest of others, and prepare to hear yes again and again.

### Congruency

Your external actions and internal thoughts must be aligned. I call this "congruency." Years ago, a Harley-Davidson dealer wanted my help increasing sales of new motorcycles at his store. So I did what consultants do: I evaluated the market, employee skills, dealership processes, and the like. Improvements could be made, but something else was wrong. When I casually asked the motorcycle sales manager what he rode, he replied, "Oh, I don't ride motorcycles. They're overpriced and dangerous."

Mystery solved.

If that sales manager didn't support what he was selling, how in the world could he convince his salespeople—not to mention his customers? If you are promoting a product, an idea, or an initiative, you need to believe in it from an ethical standpoint. And even if we were to put the ethical issue aside for a moment, if you don't believe in what you are talking about, your facial expressions and body language will give you away.

In 1966, two social scientists, Ernest Haggard and Kenneth Isaacs, filmed husbands and wives engaging in difficult conversations. Who manages the money? How should the kids be raised? All sorts of emotionally charged issues were discussed during these therapy sessions. During the exchanges, Haggard and Isaacs took notes on even the briefest facial expressions made by the couples and discovered what they called "micromomentary facial expressions"—commonly referred to today as "microexpressions." Microexpressions last between 1/5 and 1/25 of a second and typically occur during high-stakes conversations when someone has something to lose or gain, and when at least one person is attempting to suppress his or her true feelings about something. Subsequently, the other person almost always senses this disconnect.

Several years ago, my wife, Amy, and I were in the market for a new television. We went to a store that shall remain nameless (big-box, yellow sign), where we selected a new TV. Amy looked on encouragingly as a blue-shirted employee and I wrestled the monstrous set onto a large industrial cart. We suddenly found ourselves surrounded by a gaggle of salespeople who apparently had just undergone stealth training. The leader of this group began touting extended service–plan benefits to protect our purchase. The newcomers nodded in unison, as if they were backup singers in a service-plan band.

Amy and I know and believe in the value of service contracts. We've helped Harley-Davidson Financial Services increase service contract sales for years. We always buy them for our Harley-Davidson motorcycles and often get them for our cars, computers, and iStuff. However, I treat interactions with salespeople as persuasion research, and I approach that task with the zeal of an archaeologist on the verge of discovering the Ark of the Covenant.

"I thought I just selected a fantastic TV. Why would I need a service plan?" I innocently inquired. The leader of the blue shirts stammered something about how the TV is not a divine creation and that man-made objects break. Another added an almost Stallone-like "Yeah."

I hit them with objection after objection. After watching the blue-shirted team sputter, struggle, and shift back and forth, trying to find answers they didn't know, I finally revealed my background: "Guys, I help people sell extended service plans for a living."

It was as if I had suddenly flipped on a light switch, and the cockroaches scrambled. We weren't experiencing microexpressions, but rather macroexpressions. Those guys split. Almost immediately, Amy and I found ourselves alone with that gigantic TV.

Compare that exchange with one we had just days later shopping at a different retailer for a portable DVD player. After we had selected the brand and model we wanted, the young salesperson brought up the extended service plan. I could almost hear Amy's eyes rolling, as she knew what was coming next. With the confidence of Babe Ruth in a T-ball game, I began my research: "I thought we just purchased a great DVD player," I said, using my familiar refrain. "Why would we need an extended service plan?" Again, I uttered objection after objection, building up to my big reveal: "Young man," I said in my best Homer Simpson voice, "I show people how to sell extended service plans for a living."

Without missing a beat, he exclaimed, "Perfect! Then you're going to want the four-year plan."

We bought the four-year plan. Why? Because that kid believed in what he was selling. His face showed he believed. His body language was open and energetic. And his voice sounded sincere.

This is why I always say the most fundamental persuasion principle is congruency: If you want to be convincing, you have to be convinced.

* * *

Continuing our story from the beginning of the chapter: Sally Matheson knew all about reciprocity. She understood what persuasion could and couldn't do. She recognized the importance of having a healthy approach to organizational give-and-take. She also was convinced her initiative was good for the company, its customers, and Peter's department as well as her own. And, as the multimillion-dollar project's deadline loomed, she was convinced Peter Simmons felt the same way.

In his mind, Peter began replaying past experiences with Sally, much the way a high school graduation slideshow unfolds with Green Day's "Good Riddance (Time of Your Life)" as the soundtrack. Peter remembered the time Sally went to bat for him on a controversial open-source programming idea, an idea that eventually became a big success—perhaps the greatest accomplishment of his career. He recalled how they worked together almost around the clock on a secret new product—project code–named "Thor"—only to be shut down in less than five minutes by an overly conservative board of directors. Peter and Sally had worked together, won together, and lost together more times than he could count over the past five years.

He looked at Sally again, who, in her tailored blue suit and matching Christian Louboutins, radiated as much professionalism now after almost 12 hours in the office as she did when she walked in that morning. "Well?" nudged Sally. "Do you have the energy to scale Kilimanjaro again?"

"For you?" Peter responded rhetorically, letting a beat pass to heighten the drama before breaking into a massive grin. "Yes. Unequivocally, yes."

---

### Chapter 1 Persuasion Points

1. Peer-to-peer persuasion challenges can be the toughest and most frequently faced. So take a page from Sally Matheson's playbook and comport yourself for the long term.

2. *Persuasion* means "ethically winning the heart and mind of your target." Think of influence as organizational horsepower.

3. Persuasion has two primary roles: to get someone to willingly do something and to get someone to willingly *not* do something.

4. The Persuasion Paradox: While persuasion is crucial to people's success for many reasons, they actually spend very little time and effort improving their persuasion skills.

5. To get the most from this book, you must set a persuasion priority. *Who* do you want to say yes, and to *what*?

6. Persuasive people are assertive, empathetic, communicative, tenacious, and resilient.

7. *Reciprocity* means "a cooperative interchange." It's the golden thread woven through almost all aspects of persuasion.

8. The savviest professionals freely give and take.

9. The oldest methods of getting someone to buy into something are reward, punishment, and normative means. But the most powerful method is enlightened self-interest.

10. The ultimate persuasion principle is congruency. To be convincing, you have to be convinced.

# Decision Making

## The Surprising Reasons People Say Yes and No

Picking his way through the cramped ballroom, with people-filled padded chairs all askew, there was no clear route. Obstacles, however, were not this man's primary concern. On his face, you could see his mind racing—searching for what he would say once he was in front of the crowd. Few people like public speaking, but this situation seemed even more torturous than usual. He found his standing spot, turned, and faced the crowd.

"I have traveled three hours round-trip every day to attend this session. I've driven dangerous roads and in heavy traffic. You are a talented and knowledgeable group. I have learned from you, and you have learned from me. And I sure could use the money to help pay for gas. Please, *please*. Pick me!"

That scene played out in a Calgary persuasion workshop during which I asked three volunteers to vie for a single, crisp $100 bill by convincing the audience to individually award them the money. The idea: Whoever makes the most compelling case, winning the affections of the crowd, walks away with the cash and the bragging rights.

Participants are allowed to make their case in any way they deem appropriate, with one exception: They can't share the money or materially benefit the crowd in any way. (*I'll buy you all drinks!*) Adding to the pressure, I give them just four minutes to develop their case and only 25 seconds to present it.

What would *you* say if you were in this situation?

This activity mirrors business life today in many ways. You are often in competition with others for the account, the promotion, the project. You must think on your feet and be able to put together compelling arguments fast, and you might not have much time to state your case. Sometimes you need to do all this—especially in peer-to-peer persuasion situations—without offering your target some sort of material gain. Not an easy assignment, to be sure.

The most interesting aspect of this workshop activity, though, is not the people vying for the money—it's the people deciding who will earn the money. You may think that people are carefully analyzing participants' arguments, weighing the pros and the cons to rationally decide who gets their votes. That's not what's happening. At all. The surprising truth is that most people have no idea why they say yes.

## UNEXPECTED TRUTHS ABOUT YOUR THINKING

Nobel Prize–winning economist and author Daniel Kahneman suggests that human beings possess two "systems" for thinking: one that processes information very quickly, and one that does so more slowly and requires significantly more effort. Here's the thing: Most of us don't really like to think all that hard. As humans, we rely on what comes to mind with the least amount of cognitive strain. We also don't always act rationally—rarely going to the trouble of, say, doing the math or weighing the pros and cons of a particular decision.

But don't be too hard on yourself. We act that way to survive in a postmodern world where the amount of information we are exposed to has grown exponentially but the basic architecture of our brains hasn't changed since the likes of *Australopithecus africanus* roamed the earth. We employ mental shortcuts to survive. Sometimes they help; sometimes they don't.

## BEING SAVVY ABOUT HEURISTICS AND BIASES

Heuristics are supportive cognitive shortcuts that help us make good decisions in times of complexity. Biases, on the other hand, impede decision making. Sometimes, biases also are referred to as cognitive illusions because, much like an optical illusion, they twist our thinking about reality.

So how do we distinguish between the two? It's often difficult to parse heuristics and biases, because the same factors that impact our thinking also impact our thinking about our thinking. Furthermore, heuristics and biases are built into our psychological makeup and are so pervasive that we rarely even notice them working inside our heads. Plus, they feel natural, so how could they be wrong? If you make what turns out to be a good decision, you've just used a heuristic. If the decision results in a negative outcome, you succumbed to mental bias. As one psychology student so aptly put it: "Heuristics are helpful biases. Biases are hurtful heuristics."

Regardless of how you might categorize these mental patterns, understanding and labeling them will help you consider these cognitive processes more easily and create strategic persuasion campaigns based on them. They also will help your targets make better decisions. What follows are the heuristics and biases most prevalent in persuasion. Don't worry about getting too hung up on trying to determine whether something is a heuristic or a bias (even though I may use those terms in my descriptions). Simply concentrate on what these mental tendencies mean to you in terms of your persuasion efforts.

## CIALDINI'S SIX PRINCIPLES OF PERSUASION

We can't discuss persuasion and mental patterns without first talking about Robert Cialdini and his six principles of persuasion. His work is so important to the understanding of persuasion that I sometimes call him the "Ben Franklin of the Affirmative." Cialdini, now regents' professor emeritus at Arizona State University, wrote *Influence: The Psy-*

*chology of Persuasion* in 1984. (It later was published as a textbook under the title *Influence: Science and Practice*.) The original book stemmed from Cialdini's literature review of almost 50 years of scientific research regarding persuasion, plus his own ethnographic studies.

Cialdini is so highly respected in the field that he was a part of a "dream team" of behavioral scientists who helped create persuasive approaches for President Barack Obama's 2012 presidential reelection campaign. Regardless of your political leanings, Cialdini's additions were subtle and brilliant. "We know you've voted in the past . . ." was a subtle prompt known as "consistency" that convinced those who voted in 2008 to vote for Obama again in 2012. Cialdini also helped teach campaign volunteers to address rumors that Obama was a Muslim by reframing them: "Obama is not a Muslim" actually repeated the claim and reinforced it in the electorate's collective mind. "Obama is a Christian," on the other hand, reframed and refocused the discussion.

Cialdini created something akin to a "Unified Field Theory of Persuasion" by categorizing almost every persuasion approach into one of six primary principles: reciprocity, scarcity, consistency, liking, authority, and social proof. Cialdini's principles are great examples of heuristics, meaning that when we humans follow them, we typically have a good result. (There are always exceptions.) The other interesting aspect of Cialdini's principles is that they are largely social, prompted by or intensified by human interaction. Let's take a look at each principle in turn.

### Reciprocity

As noted in Chapter 1, reciprocity involves the give-and-take of human exchange. People repay others in kind. Every culture in the world teaches this principle in one way or another. When someone does something for you, it's almost embedded in your DNA to want to return that favor in kind.

Reciprocity can range from the simple and instantaneous to something much more involved and complex. Examples can be found in day-to-day life on an individual level, such as helping a coworker prepare for a presentation after he helped you prepare for yours. On a departmental level, the sales team might assist the marketing staff with some unusual but critical market data, and then marketing reciprocates by providing extraordinary support for sales. Reciprocity can even occur between competing companies: Apple and IBM announced a wide-ranging partnership in 2014 to develop business software together.

If you stop to think about it, reciprocity helps societies evolve. People inherently realize that when they do something for somebody else, they are not simply giving of their time, energy, and financial resources; they eventually will receive something in return. The best way to leverage reciprocity is to enter every situation by asking yourself, "Who here can I genuinely help?"

### Scarcity

Call it the Rule of the Rare, the Fact of the Few, or the Coefficient of the Insufficient. People want more of what they perceive to be a dwindling supply. This, too, may have derived from a survival trait.

Countless examples exist of how individuals have responded to a dwindling supply of something. One of my favorite reactions is the panic caused when Hostess Brands, the 82-year-old maker of Twinkies and other snacks, filed for Chapter 11 bankruptcy in 2012. Shoppers began stockpiling Twinkies, fearing they'd find no alternative for their sugar fixes. News outlets reported that at least one person tried to capitalize on the scare by offering a single Twinkie on eBay for $8,000!

To truly leverage the principle of scarcity, the scarcity must truly be real. There really needs to be "Only three days left!" or "Limited inventory!" Anything else, and lack of ethics comes into play. And if you think people are worried about what they might be missing, they're even more concerned about losing what they already have. That's why "loss language" (*forfeit, surrender, forgo*) is always preferable to "gain language" (acquire, obtain, secure) when playing the persuasion game.

## Consistency

What do you call someone who says one thing, yet does another? Hypocrite. Liar. Flip-flopper. Politician. Teenager. Most of these aren't exactly glowing terms of endearment.

We like, trust, and want to interact with people who follow through on what they say. When a coworker tells you he'll hand in a report by the close of business, you think highly of him when he does just that. If he doesn't, that colleague's credibility drops a notch. Similarly, when company management promises to make a change to a problematic tuition reimbursement policy that never comes, the culture in that organization shifts to the negative.

The good news is that these occurrences aren't likely to happen. Why? Once most people make a decision or take a position, especially publicly, they strive to act in accordance with that publicly stated notion. This has been proven time and time again.

## Liking

Another key found in Cialdini's work is the principle of liking. We like those who like us (and state it publicly), as well as those who are like us. Whether they have similar political views or hobbies, hail from the same part of the world, or indulge in the identical, less-than-healthy habit of smoking cigarettes, individuals with commonalities feel an affinity for one another.

I've heard the argument that respecting somebody is more important than liking somebody. Fair enough, but if you actually *like* that person, you're more willing to consider her arguments more carefully, give her more time to communicate, and be more receptive to her messages. Again, this is human nature; you just can't help it. So what is the takeaway here? Be approachable, seek similarities, and don't be afraid to pay someone a compliment every once in a while.

## Authority

We defer to experts. Whether you're a scientist, a medical doctor, a Ph.D., or a professor, if you have a level of expertise—and your target

**Simple Conversation Starters**

Take a page from bestselling author Jim Collins: Start with the question, "May I ask, where are you from?" You'll receive a host of responses, upon which you can build the rest of the conversation. Individuals may respond by mentioning a locale ("I'm from Pennsylvania."), a company ("I work at Microsoft."), an industry ("I work in the tech sector."), or even a discipline ("I'm in finance.").

Then ask an intriguing follow-up question: "How did someone from Pennsylvania end up all the way out here in California?" "What's the best aspect of life at Microsoft?" "Have you ever worked in any other industry?" "What's the most common misconception about working in the finance world?" You'll more than likely receive an engaged response, which is fantastic. Because although you're asking someone to talk about himself, your line of questioning will make *you* seem more interesting, too.

is aware of that expertise—you automatically become more persuasive. It's that simple.

If you have a title, credential, or significant certification, make it known in subtle, yet powerful, ways. Put that distinguishing credential in your email signature or post your diploma in your office. (I know a professional who once attended a prestigious executive education program, but rather than tell everyone he attended, he simply showed up at meetings with a coffee cup from that university!)

## Social Proof

And, finally, we come to Cialdini's last principle: social proof. People follow the lead of similar others, and people's tendency in this regard intensifies whenever a situation is uncertain (*Sales are down. What should we do?*) or comparable (*All the other computer companies offer package deals.*). The most powerful example of this is peer pressure among teenagers. Studies show that teens with two friends who smoke tobacco products are 1,000 percent more likely to smoke; those with three or more tobacco-toting friends are 2,400 percent more likely to smoke.

Social proof holds sway in the office, too. If you notice coworkers signing up for the United Way HomeWalk, you will be more inclined to do so. If you see that others are working late at the office, you more than likely will start setting aside a few evenings to stick around as well. If everyone appears to be on board with the new marketing direction, you will probably be on board, too—even if you're not a fan of the new marketing direction. We are social creatures.

The absolute best way to leverage social proof in a business setting is through the use of testimonials and referrals, which demonstrate that others have benefited from knowing and working with you. And now your target will, too. In Chapter 10, "Yes Success," I'll show you how to specifically make these requests. For now, just understand the power of social proof.

As they use other heuristics, people often use Cialdini's six principles, individually or in combinations, to make decisions. Now that you know them, so can you. Next, let's set our sights on understanding the most prominent biases—and learning how to navigate each of these human tendencies in turn.

## AVAILABILITY BIAS

Perhaps the root bias of all is availability. We have a tendency to give the most credence to what we can most easily recall. If we remember an occurrence quickly without much effort, we find it perfectly suited for whatever the question is before us. For examples of this, look no further than your relationship with your spouse or significant other.

People in relationships often share the burden of household responsibilities. One of the main areas of contention between couples is "fair share"—as in, "Is the other person doing his or her fair share of the chores around here?" The conflict occurs when one person believes he is doing more than the other. What might really be happening, though, is that both individuals are falling prey to the bias of availability. What you remember, and therefore exaggerate, is the last time *you* did the dishes, or *you* took out the trash, or *you* made the bed. So in your mind, you think you *always* do something, and the other person *never* does it. See any potential problems?

Availability Bias also can cause problems at the office, as your brain actually substitutes one question for another. Let's say your vice president of engineering asks you to recommend the best-qualified supplier to provide exhaust systems for your company's new engine. And in the instant of the conversation you say, "We should go with Wilson's Exhausts."

What may actually have taken place in your mind is *not* a careful analysis based on price, reliability, quality, and suitability for this particular engine. Rather, you might just recommend *any* exhaust system provider you can remember. Your brain may have substituted the question, "Who's the best?" with "Who can you name?" (And now, thanks to the Principle of Public Commitment, you've gone on record, and will now defend that selection!)

The Availability Bias also most impacts us when we are trying to gauge the relative size of a category or the frequency of an occurrence. How large is the market for red laser wall levels? (*Huge! I used one this weekend.*) How often are Wall Street traders arrested for illegal activity? (*All the time. I just read an article about another one yesterday.*)

The insufficiency of the reasoning in these examples is obvious, but it is the rare individual who would submit to the more difficult task of finding out the actual statistics that would answer either of the above questions. Many people simply don't want to work that hard. We take the path of least intellectual effort. We're human.

### Positively Leveraging Availability

How can you leverage this concept of Availability Bias to ethically win the heart and mind of your target? It's imperative to keep the value of your "ask" in front of your target. Time dims people's positive memories, so you must find ways to maintain your expertise, your value, and your shared experiences. Sending a reminder email, revisiting a key point casually in conversation, or mailing a communiqué that augments or amplifies your position all work beautifully. Remember, however, there is a distinction between keeping your contributions top of mind and . . . well, stalking. Persuasive professionals know the difference and rarely cross the line.

Frequency certainly impacts one's ability for recall, but other factors leading to Availability Bias include dramatic events (winning an important award or surviving a tragedy), intense personal experiences (receiving accolades or suffering public embarrassment), vivid descriptions (created by using language or graphics), and a notion related to frequency called the "Recency Effect" (in which people remember the last thing they heard on a topic). When you can summon dramatic public events, do so. If your company is generating positive press regarding a purchase or other strategic move, that is the time to reach out to new prospects. If someone undergoes an intense and negative experience related to your "ask" ("The trade show was terrible! I had to set up the booth until midnight, and then I had to work the show for nine hours the next day. I was exhausted when speaking with prospects."), that is the time to push for agreement on your objective ("See? This is *exactly* why I'm recommending we ask the board for budget dollars for either more head count or expanded outsourcing!").

Other tips include using vivid descriptions instead of just numbers: "The new retail space we're recommending could house AT&T Stadium," instead of "The space we're recommending is one million square feet." And, of course, before someone makes a key decision, keep the Recency Effect in mind. Literally the last thing you want the decision maker to hear is your input. People remember—and give added weight to—the final comment they've heard on the topic. You want to be the last person whispering in their ear.

# THE HALO EFFECT

Known scientifically as "Exaggerated Emotional Coherence," and more commonly as the "Halo Effect," this concept doesn't receive the attention it should. The Halo Effect occurs when we judge others positively in one aspect of their lives (appearance, wit, charm, industriousness) and then apply positive feelings to them for other, often unrelated, areas (problem solving, leadership, sales prowess).

Edward Thorndike first observed the Halo Effect and published his findings in 1920 in a paper called "The Constant Error in Psychological Ratings," which analyzed military officers' rankings of subordinates. If a soldier boasted a strong physical appearance, he also typically was considered to have impressive leadership abilities. If he was loyal, he also was rated as highly intelligent. The correlations proved way too consistent for Thorndike, who determined that officers' impressions in one area of a soldier's experience too often colored their impressions in another.

That practice holds true today. If someone is attractive, he also usually is considered smart. If a person appears enthusiastic, she often also is perceived as hard working. Friendly? Must be a good leader, too.

## Priming the Halo Pump

When it comes to evaluating people, first is always foremost. People remember the first piece of data they receive about a person, and their subsequent impressions are shaped by that data. One of the earliest and most enduring studies of first impressions and the Halo Effect was completed by Solomon Asch, who asked people to evaluate the personalities of two individuals named Alan and Ben. Asch presented the two individuals thus:

*Alan:* intelligent – industrious – impulsive – critical – stubborn – envious

*Ben:* envious – stubborn – critical – impulsive – industrious – intelligent

Obviously, the series of adjectives used to describe Alan is simply reversed for Ben. Here's the catch: Although the same words appeared in a different sequence, test subjects always viewed Alan significantly more favorably than Ben. Even Alan's negative characteristics were seen more positively, because of the positivity applied to the initial descriptors. If someone you view positively possesses a stubborn streak, you consider him a person who takes a principled stand. On the other hand, if you already have a negative impression of that person, the stubbornness can be seen as a sign of inflexibility and unwillingness to consider new ideas.

## Creating Your Halo

The clear takeaway here is to do everything you can to create a positive entry point with your target. In the earliest stages of a relationship with a target, you should dress well, be friendly and approachable, and be well read, well traveled, and conversational. You must articulate your value and add important contributions to discussions. Make a favorable impression early, and you'll dramatically improve the likelihood of hearing yes later.

Meeting an important target with whom you want to cultivate a positive and persuasive relationship? The savvy professional puts thought into not only how to make a positive impression, but also how to shape conversations. Consider the context of the meeting. Will it be a formalized business setting in a boardroom? Or will it be a more casual one-on-one exchange in an office? Conduct some research and explore similarities, interests, and unusual aspects of the target's background. Be prepared to speak intelligently about the issue at hand, ask incisive questions, and add a thought-provoking perspective. But don't overdo it and feel the need to become an expert on every potential topic to be discussed.

The Halo Effect invokes the image of concentric circles on a body of water. As long as you can make one favorable impression with someone early on, you'll build positivity in other areas of your business relationships.

**Navigating When There's No Halo**

What if you were Ben, from the Asch example? What if the first impression you leave is far from angelic? If positivity is the Halo Effect, then this opposite impression must be the "Horns Effect." Something about you is off-putting to someone else. And much like the Halo Effect, the Horns Effect can color your interactions with others.

We'll talk more about recovering your credibility in Chapter 5. For now, here is a quick way to overcome less-than-saintly impressions that involves a real Ben: Ben Franklin. Known for many things, including astute observations of human behavior and practicing persuasion, Franklin was chosen in 1736 without opposition to be clerk of the Pennsylvania General Assembly. The next year, he again was chosen. But this time, a new assembly member offered a long argument against Franklin and in support of another candidate. Franklin won out, but he found it disconcerting that the assembly member—a person of influence—rallied so publicly against him. Franklin knew he needed to win him over and didn't want to appear obsequious or servile in his approach.

So what did Benjamin Franklin do? He eventually asked his adversary if he would be so kind as to lend him a rare book from his library. Franklin was renowned for his discerning taste in books, and his target proudly agreed to lend him the requested copy. Franklin showed his gratitude with a nice note later on, and evermore the two men enjoyed a lifelong positive relationship. This episode is said to have inspired Franklin to coin this aphorism: "He that has once done you a kindness will be more ready to do you another, than he whom you yourself have obliged."

## PRESENT-VALUE BIAS

Despite what some people say, we value our present, the here and now. One way to test for this Present-Value Bias is simply to ask someone, "Which would you rather have: $100 in 365 days, or $102 in 366 days?" When faced with such a choice, most people will think (and often say),

"Well, if I can wait a year, I can certainly wait a year and a day, so I'll take the $102 in a year and a day."

On the surface, this response seems to prove that when faced with an economic choice, delayed gratification provides a better return and that people operate rationally when faced with this sort of option. What it actually does is set up a beautiful contrast. Try asking the same person this question: "Would you rather have $100 today, or $102 tomorrow?" Typically, before you even get that question out, the other person blurts, "I'll take the $100 today!" We say we understand the value of putting off immediate gratification, but we rarely act like we do.

### Leveraging Present-Value Bias

Sellers on eBay who use the "Buy It Now" feature leverage Present-Value Bias. Sure, there's a chance a buyer might be able to "win" the item for less if she waits, but she'd potentially be sacrificing (remember Cialdini's scarcity principle?) the certainty of owning the item. Another example is Amazon.com's "Buy Now with 1-Click" button. It's fast, your credit card is on file, there's no need to enter an address, and if it's a Kindle book download, you'll have your purchase in seconds. Both of these methods leverage people's tendency toward Present-Value Bias.

How can *you* leverage your understanding of Present-Value Bias to become a more effective persuasion practitioner? By making it easy for your target to say yes *right now* (easy to sign, easy to pay, easy to select) and making sure there is an immediate payoff for your target (a monetary return, a time savings, an information exchange, a reduction in labor intensity). You, too, should have a "1-Click" button.

## THE CONCEPT OF ANCHORING

When it comes to numbers, we anchor to whatever number we hear first regarding a specific topic. The new manufacturing plant will cost $35 million. The marketing initiative will take $5 million of our budget. The new training program is going to run us $550,000. Now, whenever we think of these initiatives, we will rightly or wrongly compare any cost figures with those. In fact, not only do we anchor, we compare and contrast, too.

Say, for example, you are quoted a price for a new training program. You then compare all subsequent figures you see and hear, relative to that first figure. And then another fascinating psychological occurrence happens: The principle of contrast kicks in. If the first dollar amount you were quoted was $550,000 for a training program, and the next one is $750,000, that cost seems even higher than it is, because you are comparing it with your anchor of $550,000.

If you're vying for approval on a budget and you have numbers to share, always share a range of numbers early in your communication, and make sure those numbers are generous. That way, subsequent numbers won't seem quite as high because you've already anchored your targets to a numerical set. Similarly, if you're trying to dissuade someone from following a particular route, make certain early conversations use lower numbers, which will make subsequent numbers seem even higher by comparison. When anchoring to make subsequent offers seem high (expensive) start low, to make subsequent offers seem low (affordable) start high. Remember, however, that your numbers must always be two things: real and legitimate.

## Controlling Unrelated Anchors

Another component of anchoring, one that is much more difficult to control but still worthy of consideration, is that of unrelated anchors. This can occur when numbers with no relevance to your initiative can nevertheless influence your target's thinking. In one study, participants were shown a bottle of wine and asked to estimate the highest dollar amount they would pay for that particular bottle. Before they were to write down their bid, subjects were asked to jot down the last two digits of their social security number. Those who had the highest social security number digits also bid the highest for the wine. The participants anchored to a totally unrelated number, which influenced their responses.

If you are presenting numbers for the first time in a meeting, take into consideration whether your target is being exposed to other numbers prior to your presentation. If so, those numbers could impact the perceptions of your request. If you can adjust the agenda to give your good idea the best chances of success, do so.

## CONFIRMATION BIAS

Because you're sophisticated enough to be reading this book, you more than likely are familiar with the concept behind Confirmation Bias: We seek facts, stats, and opinions that prove our hypothesis or our preconceptions. The person we hired is doing a fantastic job, the program we launched is performing exactly as intended, and the product our team created is adding what we thought it would to our market share.

Confirmation Bias can lead to poor decision making because it provides people with all the reasons to support their own claims and aims, with nothing to refute. If you're attempting to ethically win the heart and mind of your target, you must do your due diligence. Look at all relevant data sets to make sure that what you're proposing is the right thing to do. Once you're convinced that your proposal is the right thing for your target, for you, and for the surrounding situation, acknowledge the bias.

### Leveraging Confirmation Bias

Leveraging Confirmation Bias in persuasion can sound like this: "When we started this project, I wanted things to work out with the proposed new vendor. Much like the researcher who tries to prove his hypothesis, I looked for reasons we should partner with this company. I looked at locale, capacity, and all of the things that company does well. And that's exactly what I found. Reasons we *should* partner with it. But we'd be fooling ourselves if we didn't do our due diligence and ask if we're not falling prey to Confirmation Bias by seeing only what we want to see. We should spend a little more time considering this carefully and perhaps have a few others who aren't as close to the project take a look."

You'll be seen as intelligent, honest, and a person of integrity. Why? Because you are.

## ADDITIONAL COGNITIVE BIASES

As a persuasive professional, you should also be aware of the following additional biases:

| Name | Description | Example |
|---|---|---|
| Selective Recall | Remembering just those facts that prove your assumptions | *"The promotion was a success. We sold 500,000 units!"* <br><br> (But we lost money due to discounts.) |
| Base Rate Neglect | Ignoring the background statistics for compelling anecdotal information | *"Let's create a first-time buyer's program. Here are three success stories!"* <br><br> (Never mind that 87 percent of users of these programs default.) |
| Certainty Illusion | Unrealistically needing to have absolute confidence or certainty in a given action | *"I'll only green-light the project if we are certain of its success."* <br><br> (Nothing is guaranteed.) |
| Group Think | Going along with the group because of a powerful culture or perceived peer pressure | *"We've never made it work before, but we're all certain we can do it this time. You?"* <br><br> (Well, if you all think so . . .) |

*(Continued on next page)*

| Name | Description | Example |
|---|---|---|
| Overvalue Sunk Costs | Continuing to invest in lost causes by throwing good money after bad | *"We can't stop funding the initiative now. Look at how much we've spent!"* (And look at how much more you're going to spend!) |
| Gambler's Fallacy | Thinking you can beat the house; winning isn't random | *"The prospect hasn't said yes in the past six attempts; let's pitch again. We're due!"* (No, you're not.) |
| Endowment Effect | Valuing something more, because you "own" it | *"The catalog project has been ours for years. It's much too important to leave to an outside agency."* (Perhaps your contribution would be worth even more if we freed your group to do something else?) |

## EMPLOYING HEURISTICS AND
## BIASES IN EVERYDAY SITUATIONS

Understanding heuristics and cognitive biases is crucial to maximizing your persuasive potential. As stated earlier, persuasion is *ethically* winning the heart and mind of your target. You must be convinced your request is good for your company, good for you, good for your target, and good (or, at a minimum, neutral) for your industry. If those conditions are met, then the two primary persuasive purposes provided by both heuristics and cognitive biases are to:

1. *Use the momentum of mental patterns to know* **when** *to use* **what** *information.* The two obvious examples are priming and anchoring. If you want a person or a project to be perceived with a positive "halo," ensure that the first descriptors your target hears are positive, and vice versa. With anchoring you can make any number—be it a potential project cost, or potential business gain—seem either more or less by controlling the number first associated with your topic.

2. *Point out the potential harm of mental patterns.* For instance, if your target appears swayed by a compelling anecdote that is not yours, inform him of the all-too-common tendency to fall prey to Base Rate Neglect and ask him to help research facts and statistics to prove your point.

* * *

Back to the story that began this chapter: After each of the three contestants made his case for the $100 bill, I lined up the group for judging. Would the winner be the guy who claimed he risked life and limb to arrive at the workshop, but essentially just needed the money for gas? Would it be the generous man who stated he would donate the money to a charity? Or, finally, would it be the person who claimed his peers should pick him because he held his own with the group at happy hour?

To determine the victor, I used a timeless and scientific method: the applause-o-meter. When I asked for applause for the most persuasive presentation, the results were absolutely clear. The winner was our hero who needed gas money. He beamed as he received the crisp $100 bill, and the crowd gave him another thunderous round of applause. During the luncheon that immediately followed the workshop, I did what I always do: I inquired with those at my table about the contest and what they found so compelling about the winner's argument. The comments were enlightening:

*"I voted for him because he's been so helpful ever since the start of this workshop."*

*"He's always willing to run a sales simulation or brainstorm an idea, so I like him."*

*"He's so funny. He had me cracking up all morning."*

Alas, the Availability Bias and Halo Effect are alive and well and thriving in Calgary.

---

### Chapter 2 Persuasion Points

1. As humans, we use mental shortcuts called heuristics and biases.

2. Reciprocity makes us want to repay others in kind; help others and they'll help you.

3. Scarcity means we want more of what we only can have less of; when things are genuinely scarce, let people know.

4. Consistency is the fact that most people want to perform up to the level they said they would.

5. We like those who like us and are like us; find similarities with your targets and make them known.

6. The Principle of Public Commitment means if we state a decision publicly and of our own volition, we are more likely to follow through with it.

7. We defer to experts, so develop your expertise.

8. Information that most easily comes to mind is given the most consideration; be the last person whispering in your target's ear.

9. Understand both the Halo Effect and the Horns Effect; it's important to make a good impression early.

10. Anyone can leverage Present-Value Bias by making it easy to say yes now. Immediate gratification is the name of the game.

11. We anchor to the first numbers we hear and then compare other subsequent numbers with them.

12. The two fundamental ways to leverage both heuristics and biases are to understand what to say when, and to point out to your target the potential harm of certain mental patterns.

# Targets, Technology, and Tactics

## Because It's Not About You, It's About Them

Jim Morrison had it right: "People are strange."

Morrison, the late singer for the iconic 1960s band The Doors, wrote a song with that line and that title for the group's 1967 album, *Strange Days*. Why are people strange? Because they're different—in some cases, *very* different.

The people you'll be attempting to persuade—*your targets*—possess personality, gender, and generational differences as well as individual preferences. Understanding and tapping into these differences, will be pivotal to your successful persuasion efforts. They will impact how you behave, what sort of case you make, the language you use, and the references you choose.

Your targets also will have multiple and varying technological tendencies. Not everyone carries a new piece of tech in his pocket, and not everyone uses technology in the same way. Very often, such behavioral differences will be based on generational gaps. Think about it: Have you ever seen a Millennial write an actual letter on paper, or a Mature use Skype? Different technological propensities, of course, impact everything from how you communicate with your target to your target's attention span. A Boomer orders a book online and is pleasantly surprised when it lands on his doorstep 48 hours later. A Millennial orders sneakers from Amazon and wants them to magically (and instantly) appear from her smartphone.

As if those differences weren't enough, all of these factors blend together to affect your target's perception of right and wrong. Sometimes, a very fine line exists between what one person considers "ethical" and another calls "manipulation." And depending on your target, those lines of demarcation shift. Yep, it's a brave new world.

In order to embrace your future, we must return to the past—1981, to be exact, and the seminal work conducted by David Merrill and Roger Reid.

## PERSONALITY DIFFERENCES

In their book, *Personal Styles and Effective Performance* (Radnor, PA: Chilton Book Company), Merrill and Reid explain that each person has a particular social style created by the conclusions others draw about him or her and based on what he or she does and says. The very definition of *behavior* is "what we say and do, and how we say and do it." Many behavioral preferences develop when we are young, during situations when we desire to avoid tension and seek comfort. Thus, people, like chameleons, don't change their behavior as much as they change their circumstances.

Once you accurately assess another person's behavioral preferences, you can predict how he or she will respond in certain circumstances. For example, when your colleague receives a negative critique, does she redouble her efforts to prove the critic wrong? Or does she argue and rationalize her position? Chances are good that whatever the resulting behavior is, it's typical of that person. Furthermore, once you know a person's tendencies, you will be better able to anticipate (and harness) his or her natural skills. For example, a person who behaves assertively can assist you in your persuasion efforts, a levelheaded coworker can help you sort through the clutter of your ask, and the office peacemaker can negotiate differences and provide a supportive pep talk.

Merrill and Reid suggest that three measures of personality exist: assertiveness, responsiveness, and versatility. For the purpose of the current discussion, we are most concerned with assertiveness and responsiveness. Assertiveness measures how forceful a person is in his approach. (Does he ask or does he tell?) Responsiveness is the emotional dimension of personality. (Does she express her feelings or contain them?) Merrill and Reid developed four personality styles based on assertiveness and responsiveness: Driving, Expressive, Amiable, and Analytical; see Figure 3-1.

*Driving Behavior:* Results. Action. Get it done—*now*. These terms describe people, *ahem*, driven by driving behavior. They are fast decision makers who work best with those who respond in kind and move just as quickly. Driving personalities seek power and autonomy via facts and information. If these people encounter a roadblock, they will go through it and not around it.

*Expressive Behavior: Communicative* and *competitive* best describe people with expressive behavior. These individuals freely talk about their thoughts and emotions and like to involve others. They don't like to surround themselves with competitors, and they crave personal recognition. Like Drivers, Expressives act quickly. Their primary concern is the future, and they've been known to change direction midstream, demonstrating impatience. Expressives heavily weigh personal opinions—theirs and considered others'—when making decisions.

*Amiable Behavior:* Relationships and cooperation are important to Amiables. They are warm, likable, and can be prone to sentimentality. They have a tendency to take things personally, power doesn't interest them, and acceptance is paramount. Often slow movers, they will talk and consider decisions carefully with their confidants before saying yes or no. Amiables seek to minimize risk at all costs.

**Figure 3-1**     Merrill and Reid Personality Style

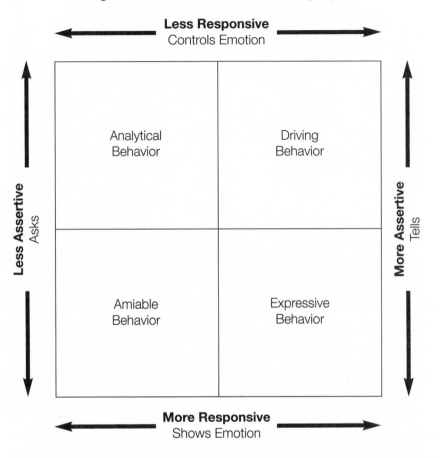

*Analytical Behavior:* You'd think all Analyticals are from Missouri. They say, "Show me the logic. Show me the principles. Show me the data. Show me the objective third-party analysis." This is the modus operandi for Analyticals. They want to know not only if something works, but how and why and who says. Others may see them as lacking energy or acting aloof, but don't be fooled: They are using their energy for mental processing and consideration of all angles of a given topic. Analyticals don't make friends easily or quickly, but once they do, relationships are important. Like Amiables, they avoid risk, because their desire to be right is almost all-consuming.

## Adapting Your Social Style for Agreement

How can you use your newfound knowledge about personality styles to hear yes more often? Cater to your target's preferences. Don't treat others the way *you* would like to be treated; treat them the way *they* want to be treated.

- *Don't small talk a Driver.* Also, share facts, not feelings, and use concision to get the decision.

- *Make an Expressive the star.* Also, resonate fun and high energy, and allow for digressions and stories.

- *Form a bond with an Amiable.* Also, take a personal interest in him, and ask for his opinion.

- *Bring out your research arsenal for an Analytic.* Also, use unqualified expert opinions, and leave no question unanswered.

The real challenge comes when *your* personality style is identical to that of your target. You'd think this would be a match made in heaven, but it isn't. A Driver working to persuade another Driver needs not only to move quickly but to double-check the details. An Expressive convincing another Expressive must be friendly and receptive while continuing to nudge the target toward the objective (see Chapter 7 for more on the Principle of Nudge). A pair of Amiables will require lots and lots of coffee. And if you're an Analytic attempting to persuade another Analytic, prepare for an exploration of the subatomic particles of your persuasion priority.

## GENDER GAPS

If you like to watch fireworks, just bring up the subject of gender differences at your friendly neighborhood cookout. Chances are the grill won't be the only thing on fire! And beware: The moment you take an absolutist stand on gender differences, you will find yourself in a proverbial gender La Brea Tar Pits.

Every individual—man or woman—has unique educational profiles, life experiences, and frames of reference. (Please keep that in mind before you send me irate emails.) That said, there is real science behind the differences between men and women when it comes to decision making and persuasion. Consider these findings:

**Men Often Overstate Their Abilities; Women Understate Them.** "In studies, men overestimate their abilities and performance, and women underestimate both. Their performances do not differ in quality," wrote Katty Kay and Claire Shipman in a lengthy article for the *Atlantic* magazine's website in 2014. The authors of *Womenomics* and authorities on gender differences in business found that women working at Hewlett-Packard applied for a promotion only when they believed they met 100 percent of the job qualifications. On the other hand, men were happy to apply when they thought they could meet 60 percent of the job requirements. *Bottom line:* Persuasion is about taking risks. You can't get the job if you don't apply.

**A Four-Letter Word for Men: Help.** In her book, *Why She Buys: The New Strategy for Reaching the World's Most Powerful Customers* (New York: Crown Business, 2009), gender expert Bridget Brennan argues that women love asking for and receiving help. For men, *help* is a four-letter word. *Bottom line:* When persuading women, offer assistance in some form. This gender preference paired with the principle of reciprocity will do wonders for you and your persuasion priority. If you're persuading men, try something like this: "I found a report that talks about what you are researching. I'll leave it here."

**Men Buy; Women Shop.** Shopping behavior mirrors gender differences throughout many aspects of life. Women consider shopping an interpersonal activity, according to Wharton marketing professor Stephen J. Hoch. Men treat it as something that must be done. *Bottom line:* Pair this idea with personality behaviors to provide an indication of how fast or slow you should move with your request.

**Women Strive for Perfectionism.** "Women feel confident only when they are perfect," wrote Katty Kay and Claire Shipman for the above-mentioned article in the *Atlantic*. "Study after study confirms that [this] is largely a female issue, one that extends through women's entire lives. We don't answer questions until we are totally sure of the answer, we don't submit a report until we've edited it ad nauseam, and we don't sign up for that triathlon unless we know we are faster and fitter than is required. We watch our male colleagues take risks, while we hold back until we're sure we are perfectly ready and perfectly qualified." *Bottom line:* No one needs to be at 100 percent all the time. In fact, no one is. Acknowledge and leverage that reality in your persuasion efforts.

**Gender Behavior Is Based on Brain Structure and Body Chemistry.** In 2006, neuropsychiatrist Louann Brizendine released *The Female Brain* (New York: Broadway Books), a book that generated major debate by claiming that women's brains "are so deeply affected by hormones that their influence can be said to create a woman's reality. They can shape a woman's values and desires, and tell her, day to day, what's important." Brizendine then released *The Male Brain* (New York: Broadway Books) in 2010, in which she states that "a man will use his analytical brain structures, not his emotional ones, to find a solution." She also notes that "the male brain thrives on competition and is obsessed with rank and hierarchy." *Bottom line:* Differences in estrogen, testosterone, and oxytocin affect mood, behavior, and the decision-making process. Everything is situational, especially this guidance. Identify the mercurial targets from among the more static and approach accordingly.

**Gender Behavior Changes with Age.** As men and women age, testosterone and estrogen levels, respectively, decrease. This results in women becoming more assertive, and men more accommodating. *Bottom line:* Take into consideration the age of your target. (Note: Generational differences are discussed further in the next section.)

**Women Don't Ask for More Money.** While researching their book *Why Women Don't Ask: The High Cost of Avoiding Negotiation—and Positive Strategies for Change* (London: Piatkus, 2007), economics professor and negotiation specialist Linda Babcock and coauthor Sara Laschever found that only about 7 percent of female MBAs attempted to negotiate their salaries when hired, compared with 57 percent of men. Those who did negotiate increased their salary by more than 7 percent. *Bottom line:* You'll never get the promotion, the assignment, the budget, or the career you want if you don't ask. The worst thing your target can say is no.

**Women Make Great Personal Evangelists.** Women focus on details, researchers say, and are more likely than men to talk to their colleagues about their experiences with you. *Bottom line:* If you want personal evangelists—people willing to sing your praises—identify women for whom you've exceeded expectations. (For more on personal evangelists, see Chapter 10.)

**Men Decide; Women Ruminate.** Scientists Colin Camerer and Read Montague imaged the brains of men and women to determine the neural roots of fidelity and betrayal. Their research found that after making a decision, the male brain turns off; female brains, however, continue to display activity in parts that regulate worry and error detection. *Bottom line:* When she says, "I have to think about it," that doesn't mean no. It usually means she *does* need to think about it.

Here are more gender differences to keep in mind:

- Women are better at negotiating for a group; men are better at negotiating for themselves.

- Men tend to avoid emotional scenes; women tend to avoid conflict situations.

- Women respond more to stories than facts; men prefer to deal in data.

Some women—and men—might be highly offended right now and argue against any generalizations like the ones listed above. Others may be nodding in knowing agreement. Despite personal sentiments, keeping these ideas in mind will help you stay out of the muck as you seek to achieve your persuasion priority.

## GENERATIONAL DIFFERENCES

"What's Omaha Beach?"

The twentysomething looked at me expectantly. I frequently tell people that not every persuasion priority should be as difficult as taking Omaha Beach. I've said it thousands of times. But this was a first. I realized I had crossed into *The Twilight Zone*. (Wait, he wouldn't know *that* reference, either!)

Yes, it seems that a mention of World War II's D-Day no longer resonates with my audiences. I've adjusted my presentations accordingly, which is what you'll need to do in your persuasion efforts. Whether you are in the cohort known as Mature or Millennial, it doesn't matter what *your* frame of reference is. You need to know your target's frame of reference.

Although the names and date ranges fluctuate among experts, here are some common generation parameters:

- Matures were born between 1909 and 1945.

- Boomers were born between 1946 and 1964.

- Generation Xers were born between 1965 and 1981.

- Millennials were born between 1982 and 2003.

The newest generation, born in 2004 and beyond, has yet to be classified with a catchy name, but no doubt one will pop up soon.

*Rocking the Ages: The Yankelovich Report on Generational Marketing*, by J. Walker Smith and Ann Clurman (New York: HarperBusiness,

1997), summarizes some of the key differences among age-groups exceptionally well. In short, Matures often are described as both the Silent Generation and the Greatest Generation, as they are defined by the idea of answering a call to duty. They celebrated victory after hard-fought battles (like the one waged on Omaha Beach) and needed to be (and still are) team players. For Matures, education was a privilege. Well-known Matures include Betty White and Don Rickles.

For Boomers, individuality reigns supreme. Youth is valued and self-absorption rampant. They feel they've been rewarded because they deserve it, and leisure is their primary reason for living. Education was an entitlement, "now" is more important than "later," and money is meant to be spent. Living examples: Bill Gates, Demi Moore, and Jerry Seinfeld.

For Generation Xers, success usually means having two jobs. And if you really want to get ahead in the world, you must be an entrepreneur. After all, "the man" exists to bring you down. Mention a "program" to Generation Xers, and they'll wonder if you're referring to Microsoft Word or Outlook Express. Living examples: Jennifer Aniston and David Beckham.

Millennials grew up in what some call the "Era of the Child." While in previous generations children were seen and not heard, this generation of kids was put on a pedestal. They typically work well with friends and on teams because they grew up with play dates and other organized social outings. They believe everyone should be rewarded for their efforts and do something not because the boss said so but because it makes sense. Millennials often are called "digital natives" because they are members of the first generation not to know what it was like to live without the Internet. Living examples: Mark Zuckerberg, Justin Bieber, LeBron James, and Kate Upton.

One generation always seems to like to mock the others. Matures pick on Boomers. Boomers make fun of Generation Xers. And everyone snipes at Millennials. It's like living in Wisconsin and making fun of people from Illinois. Easy.

## Being Savvy About Generational References

The more you know about your target's age and corresponding cultural references, the more appropriately (and successfully) you'll be able to speak persuasively with that person. What follows are key decision-making triggers that drive each generation to act:

- Matures: It's the right thing to do.

- Boomers: It feels good.

- Generation Xers: You'll get ahead if you do it.

- Millennials: It's just smart to do.

Now, people don't always look as old (or as young) as they actually are, so sometimes it can be tough to determine which generation you're dealing with. Short of embarrassing yourself and your target, how can you learn his or her age? Start by asking where and when the person went to high school. (I always seem able to work that into just about any conversation.) Tuck that info away for a future, generationally appropriate, reference. For example, with a Class of 1970 grad, you might say: "Man, that idea is going to be the Sony Walkman of your industry." But with a Class of 2005 grad, try: "It's important we keep the new product under wraps until the introduction. We don't want to be another Wiki-Leaks victim." Of course, these examples won't always resonate, but when they do, you'll see a spark in your target's eye. Besides, you don't have to be a 1970 grad to understand the Walkman reference.

Generational differences matter. One Harley-Davidson dealer I know casually asks customers during the purchase process for the name of their favorite song in high school. Then when the customer takes delivery of his or her motorcycle, guess what song is booming through the sound system? It creates strong, positive feelings about the experience and improves customer satisfaction scores. Grocery stores are masters at this. They can tell what generation is shopping when and play Muzak from roughly when that generation came of age, so they shop longer.

A number of years ago while visiting good friends, one of their twin boys—who was about 10 years old at the time—asked me if I like music. "Absolutely," I replied.

"Do you know a song called 'Slow Ride,' by a band called Foghat?"

"I know 'Slow Ride,'" I said. (It was my favorite song . . . in 1975!) "But how do you know 'Slow Ride'?"

He gave me a two-word answer: "*Guitar Hero.*"

Technology has become a game changer for generational frames of reference. It can be a game changer for your persuasion efforts, as well, which is why it is so important to use it deliberately. Which brings us to . . .

## TECHNOLOGY AND PERSUASION

We've come a long way since the carrier pigeon and town crier—and even since the postman and pen pals. That's why it is crucial to understand the role technology plays in making your persuasion priority a success.

Typically, when people discuss the intersection of technology and persuasion two concepts—HCI (Human-Computer Interaction) and CMC (Computer-Mediated Communication)—get top billing. Scientist B. J. Fogg studies how people interact with their computer devices and how their behavior subsequently changes. (For example, what effect does the MyFitnessPal app, which makes it easier to log foods by scanning the items' bar codes, have on healthful behaviors and weight loss? This is classic HCI—and it is fun stuff!) However, for our purposes, I want to focus on CMC—and, more specifically, how we use text messaging, email, and videoconferencing to be more effective and more persuasive communicators.

### Getting the Most Out of Technologically Mediated Communication

Technology has changed every aspect of our lives. It has even created new psychological phenomena, such as FOMO. People are compulsively checking their social media for "Fear of Missing Out" on some detail of their social network contacts' lives. So *you* don't miss out on how to use these new tools for maximum benefit, here are some facets of Computer-Mediated Communication you should keep in mind:

**Acknowledge That Your Target's Attention Is Fragmented.** Despite its advantages, technology has arguably emerged as the single greatest factor in rapidly declining attention spans worldwide. As contemplative computing expert Alex Soojung-Kim Pang wrote in his 2013 book, *The Distraction Addiction: Getting the Information You Need and the Communication You Want, Without Enraging Your Family, Annoying Your Colleagues, and Destroying Your Soul* (New York: Little Brown) (see, you almost couldn't keep your attention focused on that long subtitle!), humans, over the course of a typical day, send and receive an average of 110 messages, check their phones 34 times, and visit Facebook five times. People also spend 43 minutes each day waiting for devices to start up, shut down, open files, load software, or connect to the Web. Some people with type A personalities might multitask while they wait for their laptops to fire up, but you can be sure they're not fully engaged in whatever they're doing. Their attention is divided; they can't focus on any one thing for longer than a few seconds. That's why Twitter use has reached unimaginable heights, 140 characters at a time, soaring past 200 million users in fewer than seven years.

**Remember That Concision Is King.** Say it with less—in your presentations, your phone calls, and your pitches—and make your opens and closes sharp. My favorite example of concision comes from an old drive-in movie marquee that read: "Closed for Season. Reason? Freezin."

**Get It Right.** When you're persuading with facts, use data that people can easily reference. And if someone throws you a curveball, you can confidently respond with a casual, "Yes, but what that research doesn't take into account is . . ." Wham. You're in charge. And as we learned earlier, people defer to experts!

**Make It Easy.** It's imperative to remove any barriers that prevent your target from interacting with you. So include your business cell phone number in your email signature as a hyperlink. Your email recipients will be one click away from reaching out to you.

**Make It Fast.** Online companies with a "live chat" feature understand the value of "now." Customers get their questions answered and their problems solved on their schedules. This is now the standard of service. Plus, any online company worth its salt is using an optimizer to scan the conversations for patterns and buzzwords so the company can perfect its pitch. Is your personal responsiveness holding up to this level of tech?

**Opt for Synchronous Communication.** Communication can be either synchronous or asynchronous. For instance, during a videoconference one or more of your targets will hear your message at the same time. However, if you send an email blast, your targets will open it at different times in different environments. Why is this important? When trying to persuade groups of people (which we'll cover in Chapter 8), it's easier to shape opinion and persuade via synchronous communication.

**Keep Up Appearances.** Videoconferencing is here to stay, via Google Hangouts, GoToMeeting, Skype, and other services, which means you'd better check what you're wearing and where you're sitting. In 1960, when presidential candidates John F. Kennedy and Richard Nixon participated in the first-ever televised debate, Kennedy wore makeup, looking poised and confident. Nixon didn't wear makeup, and he appeared sickly and sweaty on camera. Who won that election? On videoconference days, wear what looks good on a web cam, comb your hair, add appropriate lighting, check to make sure the background isn't questionable, and by all means position the camera at a flattering angle. That up-the-nose shot doesn't flatter anyone!

**Know Text-Speak.** You may have heard about the woman who was trying to express sympathy and support to a friend who had recently lost a loved one with a text message reading "LOL." She thought the abbreviation stood for "lots of love"—not "laugh out loud." Oops. Adapt to the language of the technology. Learn abbreviations and understand emoticons.

**Use Emoticons Wisely.** Research suggests that women are twice as likely as men to use emoticons in text messages, and they often are intended to soften the blow of criticism or bad news. Men, when they do use them, pull from a wider variety of emoticons and employ them to express sarcasm.

### Defining Your Target-Specific Communication Strategy

Today, effective persuasion communication requires that you be faster, more concise, and more provocative than ever before. To sum up the chapter thus far, allow me to present a strategic persuasion prompt. To begin formulating your laser-sharp communication efforts, ask yourself the following question:

> How do I persuade a _____ (*gender*) _____ (*personality style*) and _____ (*generation*) when asking for _____ (*time, dollars, insight,* or *help*) and communicating primarily through _____ (*text, phone, face-to-face*)?

Your filled-in blanks might pose the question like this: "How do I persuade a male Driver and Generation Xer when asking for additional head count and communicating primarily through face-to-face meetings?" Your answer might be: Use a communication strategy that is fact-based and cuts to the chase about how your efforts will give him an advantage over the competition and make him look like Tom Cruise in *Top Gun.*

## PERSUASION TACTICS

Our final focus in this chapter is on persuasion *tactics*—those approaches deemed to cross the fine line between ethical persuasion and manipulation. That line of demarcation is fine precisely because it's dependent on the target's perspective. What Boomers call "selling out," Gen Xers see as corporate sponsorship, and Millennials view as the ultimate objective.

Some tactics are blatantly unethical. Watch *The Wolf of Wall Street*, and you'll see prime examples of self-interest, greed, and capitalism run amok. Bilking someone out of his life savings for worthless investment schemes is an obvious breach of legal and ethical boundaries. (The real "Wolf of Wall Street," Jordan Belfort, now sells his secrets in an "education" package called the "Straight Line Persuasion System.")

Here are some shades-of-gray approaches that marketers use in their attempts to persuade you and others:

- Amazon makes recommendations based on your prior purchases. Too intrusive?

- Advertisements for items you've Googled start showing up in your email and browser window. Invasion of your privacy?

- GPS location technology aligns with your shopping preferences to target you for promotions as you walk down the street. Tech gone too far?

- Walmart displays prepaid phone cards at the end of diaper aisles, because young mothers feel a strong desire to stay in touch with family and friends. Taking advantage?

Persuasion tactics don't seem so black or white now, do they?

### What This Means to You

Sometimes people are so afraid of acting unethically in their persuasion efforts that they fail to take *any* action and, no surprise, manage to not persuade at all. One of my mentors, the late corporate performance expert Joel DeLuca, conducted research on more than 11,000 people in nine organizations between 1974 and 2005, exposing these fears and compiling details about their behavior.

DeLuca discovered that 80 percent of the people he observed could be considered "idealists." They were hard working and well intentioned, but they made relatively little impact on the overall organization. That's because they suffered either a moral mental block or an entitlement mental block—especially in their persuasive efforts. A moral block suggests that it's somehow wrong to "work" the system to get their pitch approved. The entitlement block convinces people that "folks should do it my way" and, therefore, blindly agree with them.

The other 20 percent of people in DeLuca's research were classified as "pragmatists." They had the highest impact on their organizations, seeing them not as they wished they were, but as they actually *were*. They understood that no matter how brilliant their ideas were, they needed to make an effort to turn those ideas into realities—which meant taking action.

### Ethical Persuasion Guidelines

If the means are ethical and the ends are ethical, then you're obviously operating in an ethical manner. If, by pursuing your persuasion priority, good things will happen for your target, your company, and you, why not? This is the enlightened self-interest we talked about in Chapter 1. If, however, your means are unethical and your ends are unethical— you fabricated vendor research to steer your company to an unqualified supplier because said supplier gave you Super Bowl tickets, let's say— then you've transformed into a slimy character worthy of *Wolf of Wall Street* status.

The dilemma occurs when the ends are ethical, but the means are questionable. Consider stealth marketing. For a well-publicized 2002 covert marketing campaign initiated by Sony Ericsson to promote its new camera phone, the company hired 60 actors to pose as travelers in 10 cities and ask passersby to take their picture. Upon handing a chosen individual the new phone, the actors then casually pointed out how to use the phone and subtly mentioned some of its most impressive features, effectively giving a soft sales pitch. Marketers stressed that they wanted the exchange to feel natural.

Is this an example of an ethical means to an ethical end? To paraphrase DeLuca: "If they knew what you were trying to do, would they let you?" The "they" in the above example is the target and other key decision makers (not the competitors). So if your target knew you were trying to get the best reaction possible to your product, and that meant in a so-called natural exchange on the street, would your target still play along? Yes, probably. But if you must think about it twice, run the scenario through your head again.

I mentioned the great work of Daniel Pink earlier. In his book, *To Sell Is Human: The Surprising Truth About Moving Others* (New York: Riverhead Books, 2012), he offers a powerful rule of thumb for operating ethically: Treat everyone as you would your grandmother.

## PUTTING IT ALL TOGETHER

In this chapter, we've covered how to increase your likelihood of persuasion success by treating your targets not as you want to be treated, but as they want to be treated. Understanding personalities, gender differences, and generational gaps is crucial, as is knowing how different people view and respond to technology. And, finally, make certain everything you do—in the target's mind as well as your own—is rooted in ethically strong motives.

"People are strange," goes The Doors' song. "When you're a stranger," the line continues. However, the more you know about your targets, the less strange they will seem. Keep your target's perspective in mind as you work through the chapters to come.

## Chapter 3 Persuasion Points

1. Key to persuasion success is not seeing your target as strange, but rather as a person with different inclinations and perspectives.

2. People have a tendency to either ask or tell, to respond or not. These are two powerful planes in which personalities operate.

3. When responding to the situation you are in, act like a chameleon and be ready for whatever comes your way.

4. Men and women operate differently. Acting as if they don't is just silly.

5. For some reason, gender conversations evoke strong sentiments. Think deeply, listen intently, and avoid too many absolutist gender stands.

6. Every generation has a different frame of reference. For Millennials a "45" has always been a gun and never a record, and Elton John was never a rock star.

7. Technology changes quickly, but people don't. To maximize persuasion success you have to blend human tendencies (attention span, social needs, etc.) with technological capabilities.

8. People have different perspectives on tactics. Ask yourself, "If they knew what I was trying to do, would they let me?" If you can respond with a yes, that means you're headed in the right direction.

# Building Your Business Case

**Creating the Logical and Emotional Foundations of Your Argument**

We've covered the crucial background information: persuasion fundamentals, decision making, and key aspects about your target. The next several chapters will cover what I call your "Persuasion Equation." This is the combination of factors that will result in a rocket-fueled approach to you getting agreement.

Your Persuasion Equation is:

(A Great Business Case + Your Outstanding Credibility + Compelling Language) × Intelligent Process = Yes Success

In this chapter, we'll focus on building your business case. This is a great way of performing your due diligence to ensure your persuasion priority makes good sense for you and your target. It's also a good time to get to know more about your target. Going through this process will give you the content you need to convincingly make your appeal to others.

A solid business case requires two primary building blocks: logic and emotion (Logos and pathos for you Aristotle fans). The old saw, "Logic makes you think, and emotion makes you act," has been around so long for a reason: It works! Let's first take a look at logic.

Logic has many components: deductive reasoning, inductive reasoning, abductive reasoning, just to mention a few. But this isn't an abstruse exploration in navel gazing, so we won't spend time making philosophical arguments for how many angels can dance on the head of a pin. In business, if you want to appeal to logic, you do so with quantifiable measurements. That's right, numbers.

## QUANTITATIVE REASONING

Evaluation of numerical data is crucial when building a compelling business case. (Hey, I never promised there wouldn't be *any* math in this book!) Stick with me here; you'll be glad you did.

To be successful in business today, financial literacy is a must. You'll never reach your persuasive potential if you are terrified of your calculator. You need to know how to read and understand the basics of an income statement, a cash flow statement, and a balance sheet. You also should appreciate that, like persuading your target, working with financial figures can be an interpretive art form.

Here's what I mean: Let's say you work for a bio-friendly consumer products company that makes natural surface cleaners like you might use in your kitchen. Now, let's say you invested $100,000 in a marketing initiative that generated $1,000,000 in kitchen cleaner sales. Was your return $1 million, or was it $900,000? Or maybe it was yet another number? What do *you* think? Well, actually, the answer depends on who's doing the math!

Nonfinancial types often have trouble grasping financial disciplines, because many think of them in terms of black and white. Accounting is not an exact science; many gray areas exist. Financial reporting and forecasting are open to interpretation, judgment, and approximation, as are generally accepted accounting principles (GAAPs). In the example above, salespeople may claim a return of $1 million, the marketing team may argue the return is $900,000, and your accounting group may have other ideas. We'll talk more about this in a bit.

Seemingly simple ideas such as revenue (which in some organizations is called "sales revenue" or "gross revenue") aren't etched in stone. For example, when is that revenue "recognized" (an accounting term meaning "counted")? Is it when the purchase order is signed, when the goods are delivered, when the invoice is sent, or when the money hits the company's bank account? See? Ambiguities open up multiple interpretations.

Much like social and corporate culture norms, financial norms must be determined and adhered to. More than likely, you won't have sole responsibility for actually performing the following calculations for your company (that's what financial analysts are for), but you should have the financial literacy to know how numbers are generated and what they mean. When you do, you'll be able to speak the language of finance, ask more insightful questions, and use that information to create more compelling quantitative cases for your persuasion priorities.

As you build each case, consider as many positive aspects as you can: If your initiative could boost product market share in the Northeast by 8 percent, what might it do in other regions? Are there international implications as well? And don't forget multiplicity. If your idea would increase employee efficiency, thereby saving the company dollars, make sure you apply that savings to as many people as appropriate. Are there tangential benefits? If you sell more of product A, will increased sales of product B follow? To increase the persuasiveness of your case, consider all the benefits.

If you internalize the ideas in this section, I guarantee you'll be in the top 10 percent of all professional persuaders.

### Return vs. Return on Investment (ROI)

Here's the first financial aspect that has the potential to be confusing: What's your initiative's worth to the organization? You may hear some people say, "What's the ROI?," to which another person responds, "One million dollars." Well, that's not *exactly* accurate.

ROI, by definition, is always a ratio. Some kind of "return" or "profit" divided by the investment that generated said return. As described above, many people think of the *return* portion of ROI as the ROI, but this is technically incorrect. You don't need to point out that those people are wrong; just understand that when someone claims the ROI as a particular dollar amount, he's talking about just the *return* portion of the "return on investment."

**Dollars Returned.** When talking about just the dollars returned, the calculation is pretty straightforward: How much did you invest, and how much did you receive in return? Let's use our earlier example: You invested $100,000 in a marketing campaign, which in turn generated $1 million in sales, or gross revenue.

Gross revenue ($1 million) – marketing costs ($100,000) = dollars returned ($900,000).

Simple, right?

Well, we're not quite finished, because we haven't taken into consideration the costs of goods sold (CoGs). The most obvious CoGs are wholesale costs required to produce or acquire a product, as well as sales commissions from selling that product. What must you pay to sell the item? Your project may or may not have CoGs, depending on whether it's a product or a service. But if CoGs are involved, it is imperative you include these costs in your calculations.

So, let's crunch the numbers again with this perspective in mind, assuming that our CoGs to produce and sell are $500,000:

$$(\text{Gross Revenue } - \text{ CoGS}) - \text{Marketing Investment}$$
$$= \text{Dollars Returned}$$

$$(\$1 \text{ million } - \$500,000) - \$100,000$$
$$= \$400,000 \text{ returned}$$

The dollars returned in this example can be considered gross profit. If you want to appear reasonable, conservative, and responsible to senior management, use the gross profit number as the basis for your dollars returned. Now what about ROI?

### Return on Investment (ROI)

As mentioned earlier, ROI by definition is always a ratio; that's the "on investment" part. A ratio demonstrates the quantitative relationship between two numbers, showing how many times one number contains the other. ROI establishes the relationship between the return and the initiative's investment. In our example above, the project has a $400,000 return and a $100,000 investment. With RO I, the most elegant way to write this is with a colon, which can simply be expressed as ratio of 4:1.

Typically, when using ROI ratios, whatever you invest is always simplified to 1. But the *return* can be shown in fractional amounts. So, if the marketing campaign example above cost $150,000 (instead of $100,000), you would simply divide $400,000 by $150,000 and find the quotient to be 2.666 (which we round up to the nearest tenth, making it 2.7). That makes your ROI ratio 2.7:1. That number is not as compelling as our original example, but it's still not a bad return!

**ROI as a Percentage.**  Expressing return as a percentage is even more common and, perhaps, even more persuasive. Let's go through the steps, using the same figures as in our previous example:

*Step 1:* Calculate gross profit, as above.

$$(\text{Gross Revenue} - \text{CoGS}) - \text{Marketing Investment}$$
$$= \text{Return}$$
$$(\$1 \text{ million} - \$500,000) - \$100,000$$
$$= \$400,000$$

*Step 2:* Divide the gross profit by your investment amount to determine a factor.

$$\$400,000 \div \$100,000 = 4$$

*Step 3:* Multiply that factor by 100 and express the return as a percentage.

$$4 \times 100 = 400\%$$

Why is it more persuasive? Think back to our conversations about mental impressions; 400 percent seems like a much larger number than 4:1!

Obviously, you want a positive ROI number. However, some companies go so far as to specify ROI minimums before they take on a project. If your ROI number is negative, regardless of whether your priority is good for you personally, it's no good for your organization, and you should reconsider.

**ROI and Return Challenges.** The challenge with return and ROI calculations is establishing what's included and what isn't on both sides of the equation—the costs and the benefits. Do you calculate the hours spent by salaried employees who worked on your initiative and include that as a cost? Do you attempt to quantify improved morale and represent that as a benefit? With return and ROI, like all measures, it's valuable to consider all reasonable inclusions and exclusions. And as already stated, every company has different ways of looking at the numbers.

One final note about return and ROI calculations: If you use these calculations to forecast anticipated ROI, you may want to run a few different scenarios, such as these: What if sales are off by a particular percentage? What if the cost of goods sold is higher than anticipated? What if the product launch is delayed? Taking into consideration multiple obstacles will show others in your organization that you've done your due diligence and thought through your persuasion priority.

Now, let's talk about projects that might require capital expenditures (buildings, machines, tooling). Staying with the example of a biofriendly consumer products company, imagine you've developed a successful kitchen cleaner product and now want to pair it with biofriendly paper towels. How might you best frame your arguments? Here are a few ideas.

## Payback Period

As its name suggests, a payback period is the length of time it takes an organization to recoup its costs on an initiative. Let's say your persuasion priority is to obtain approval from your executive team to bring to market a new kind of eco-friendly paper towel (affectionately dubbed internally as the "Owl Towel"). It uses recycled materials and is more absorbent than others on the market, and you think it will do good things for both your company and the environment.

Working with all the necessary parties, you've estimated that the cost of bringing this new product to market would be $1 million. Once to market, you're estimating the Owl Towel's yearly revenues will be $350,000 for at least the next four years.

To determine the payback period, simply divide the investment ($1 million) by $350,000. This straightforward calculation tells you that your payback period on the Owl Towel will be 2.86 years. This payback calculation is useful, fast, and easy to communicate. Thus, it is a solid way of looking at your initiative. The bad news is that it does have some limitations. Why? Because $350,000 four years from now may not be worth what it is today. Here's where a financial tool called Net Present Value comes in.

## Net Present Value (NPV)

Net Present Value reflects what your multiyear project is worth in today's dollars. It answers the question: What is this cash stream really worth to the organization? To understand Net Present Value (NPV), we need to break down the term to its two component parts: "net" and "present value." If you subtract your initiative's total outgoing cash flow from your initiative's total incoming cash flow, the remainder will be your "net." Now, because of costs of capital, earning potential, inflation, and so forth, tomorrow's money is worth less than today's money is. (Ever heard the expression, "A million dollars isn't what it used to be"?) The "present value" part of this calculation (also sometimes referred to as "PV") enables us to make decisions about longer-term initiatives using a notion we can wrap our heads around: today's dollars.

To calculate Net Present Value, start by using what is known as a "discount rate." This is the rate at which future earnings for your project are, well, discounted. Unless you are currently a financial analyst for your company, you're going to need input from others on what an appropriate discount rate should be. Without expert guidance, you could do more harm than good for your idea and your reputation. The other reason you'll need guidance from your company's financial analysts is that some organizations use different discount rates for different kinds of projects (high-risk vs. lower-risk, for instance), and some even vary the discount rate based on the term of the initiative.

Let's look at NPV by building our Owl Towel financial case for the executive team: We know it will cost $1 million to bring it to market, and we conservatively estimate that we'll realize a payback of $350,000 per year. A trusted colleague in the company's finance group suggests we use a discount rate of 8 percent (0.08).

I'm going to walk you through what some might call the "old-school" way of making calculations, but I'm doing so to help you completely understand the calculation. Then we can talk shortcuts.

First, we will use our discount rate to find a discount "factor." This is the factor you will use to determine the *current* value of the money realized by your new Owl Towel. The equation to determine your discount factor is:

$$1 \div (1 + r)^t$$

with $r$ representing your discount rate, and $t$ representing the number of years. For example, our discount factor equation for the first year of our Owl Towel project would be $1 \div (1 + .08)^1$. This means 1 divided by 1.08, which equals .9259259 (of course, when rounded to the nearest thousandth—which is accurate enough for this illustration—would be .926). So to find out the Present Value (PV) of our first year's Owl Towel earnings, we multiply the cash flow of $350,000 by .926 to discover that the Present Value of our Year One earnings would be worth $324,100.

And, just so you get the hang of this, we'll do one more. The calculation for the second year of our Owl Towel project would be $1 \div (1 + .08)^2$. The superscript is stating 1.08 to the second power, which is mathematical shorthand for 1.08 x 1.08. If you multiply 1.08 by 1.08, you get 1.1664. Divide 1 by 1.1664 to get .857. This is your discount factor for Year Two. Multiply $350,000 by .857, and you'll see that the second-year Owl Towel cash flow is worth $299,950. (See how quickly the value drops? This is why Net Present Value is such an important calculation to know!) Continue using this formula for each year of your forecast.

Of course, doing the math to determine your discount factor is considered antiquated, but you should know how it works. A quick Google search for "Discount Factor Tables" or "Net Present Value Tables" is an easy way to obtain the discount factors you'll need. Here are all the calculations for our Owl Towel NPV example:

| Discount Rate: 8 Percent | | | | | | |
|---|---|---|---|---|---|---|
| | Year 0 | Year 1 | Year 2 | Year 3 | Year 4 | Totals |
| Cash Flow | ($1,000,000) | $350,000 | $350,000 | $350,000 | $350,000 | $1,400,000 |
| Discount Factor | 1 | .926 | .857 | .794 | .735 | |
| PV Cash Inflow | | $324,100 | $299,950 | $277,900 | $257,250 | $1,159,200 |
| Cash Outflow | ($1,000,000) | | | | | ($1,000,000) |
| Net Present Value | | | | | | **$159,200** |

You'll note that the total Present Value of the Owl Towel project is projected to be $1,159,200. Subtract today's $1 million investment, and the NPV of the Owl Towel proposal is actually $159,200. That is what your project is worth in terms of today's dollars.

As you can see, the Net Present Value is a more accurate indicator of Return on Investment than payback calculation is. In our previous example, which ignored the time value of money, we forecasted the payback period to be slightly less than three years. Now we know from using NPV that we really won't see payback on the project until sometime between Years Three and Four. Depending on the threshold of acceptable payback for your company, you may have to do more work to build your case. (Another term you should be familiar with here is *hurdle rate*, which is the minimum return your company will accept on an initiative before investing in it. Sometimes the discount rate and the hurdle rate are the same number.) Your credibility will skyrocket when you can demonstrate to others that you understand these powerful financial concepts and factor them into your business cases. Want to get *really* great? Wrap your mind around IRR.

## Internal Rate of Return (IRR)

Internal Rate of Return is a measure related to Net Present Value and answers this question: What rate of return will the organization receive on this project? The resulting number can be used internally to compare projects and make informed decisions, such as whether your case is strong enough to convince the organization to say yes.

In its simplest form, the Internal Rate of Return (IRR) is the interest rate necessary to make your Net Present Value zero. You do that by applying a discount factor to each year and then summing your return. How do you know what rate to use? Well, this is going to sound crazy, but you guess.

So let's go back to the Owl Towel example and try 10 percent. (A discount factor table supplies the necessary discount factors.)

| Discount Rate: 10 Percent | | | | | | |
|---|---|---|---|---|---|---|
| | Year 0 | Year 1 | Year 2 | Year 3 | Year 4 | Totals |
| Cash Flow | ($1,000,000) | $350,000 | $350,000 | $350,000 | $350,000 | $1,400,000 |
| Discount Factor | 1 | .909 | .826 | .751 | .683 | |
| PV Cash Inflow | | $318,150 | $289,100 | $262,850 | $239,050 | $1,109,150 |
| Cash Outflow | ($1,000,000) | | | | | ($1,000,000) |
| Net Present Value | | | | | | **$109,150** |

In the bottom-right cell, this calculation at 10 percent shows the NVP as $109,150. Well, that's not zero, so guess again. Let's try 14 percent.

| Discount Rate: 14 Percent | | | | | | |
|---|---|---|---|---|---|---|
| | Year 0 | Year 1 | Year 2 | Year 3 | Year 4 | Totals |
| Cash Flow | ($1,000,000) | $350,000 | $350,000 | $350,000 | $350,000 | $1,400,000 |
| Discount Factor | 1 | .877 | .769 | .675 | .592 | |
| PV Cash Inflow | | $306,950 | $269,150 | $236,250 | $207,200 | $1,019,550 |
| Cash Outflow | ($1,000,000) | | | | | ($1,000,000) |
| Net Present Value | | | | | | **$19,550** |

Here the NPV is $19,550. That's not zero, either!

I know what you're thinking as you grab your head in anguish: *Not more calculations!* I'll cut to the chase. The discount rate that turns your Owl Towel NPV calculation to zero here is 14.97 percent. Now, in some weird world of terminology that only CPAs understand, that discount rate you used to determine your discount factor now becomes your Internal Rate of Return. So your Owl Towel project has an IRR of 14.97 percent. IRR is an excellent way for internal decision makers to evaluate the financial merits of several projects at one time while also giving the organization a common way of speaking about a project.

How did I obtain such a precise IRR of 14.97 percent? Simple: I used an online IRR calculator. We live in a terrific age of technology, and you should take advantage of online calculators for their speed and accuracy. But, much like the spelling atrophy that sets in after relying on spell-check for too long, you won't be fit to make a great financial case if you don't occasionally flex your mathematical muscles. That's why I took you through the math. But the real reason is to truly understand the persuasive power of a compelling quantitative case. See how the pieces come together, like individual shards of glass creating a grand mosaic?

Knowing these numbers, you're better prepared to make your case for the Owl Towel to others. This is very likely one of those situations in which your financial case is strong but not overwhelming. So if you truly believe in this project and want to make the Owl Towel a reality, you'll need to incorporate qualitative persuasion tools, such the ones we discuss later in this chapter. But before we do that, there is one other tool I'd like to share with you: breakeven calculations.

## Breakeven Calculations

The breakeven calculation answers the question, "How many units do we need to sell to recoup our investment?"

For example, say your persuasion priority is to convince the buyer of a large retail grocery chain to carry Owl Towels. You want to offer them 100 pallets of Owl Towels at a special price of $14,000 each. You know that it will cost the chain $1,000 in expenses (shipping, stocking, commissions) to sell the towels on each pallet, and a single pallet of Owl Towels will retail for $20,000. How many pallets will the chain need to sell in order to break even?

For this example, you would first calculate your buyer's initial investment and then divide that by the gross revenue (i.e., total cash inflow) of one unit sold at full retail.

Your buyer's initial investment, therefore, is calculated thus:

$$\text{Price Per Pallet} \times \text{Number of Pallets} = \text{Initial Investment}$$

$$\$14,000 \times 100 = \$1.4 \text{ million}$$

(This is referred to as a fixed cost.)

Next, find what is referred to as a "contribution margin." How many dollars will your buyer have left after he sells your product? Here, if the retailer were to sell a pallet of Owl Towels for $20,000 and subtract $1,000 in expenses, the per pallet contribution margin is $19,000.

Finally, all that's left to do is to divide that $1.4 million fixed cost by the $19,000 contribution margin to determine that the breakeven point for this opportunity is 73.68 pallets—or said more simply, 74 pallets. Breakeven calculations are valuable because they can help keep an organization headed toward a recognizable goal. The breakeven calculation is a favorite of sales and marketing teams because it simplifies the objective and acts as a powerful persuader; everything after the breakeven point is profit!

## What It All Means

To reemphasize one of my earlier points: If you learn the above measures and can use them to build a business case for any initiative, you'll be in the 90th percentile for global business acumen. Business today is all about becoming smarter, faster. And financial literacy is essential to the persuasive business professional. If you want to be taken seriously, you'll want to speak the financial language of your organization.

That being said, never position yourself as something you are not. If you are not a financial expert, do not purport to be one. It is perfectly okay (in fact, it is encouraged) to say such things as, "I'm no financial expert, and we should certainly have the finance guys review these numbers. But my back-of-the-envelope calculations tell me . . ."

Better yet, establish relationships with your colleagues in the finance department and swing by their offices to see what they think. "You're the experts," you can honestly say. "Tell me what you think about this initiative from a numbers perspective." Then invite them to your next meeting!

Numbers are important—absolutely. But for many the *real* power of persuasion lies on the emotional side of your appeal. As Albert Einstein said: "Not everything that can be counted counts, and not everything that counts can be counted." Consider this your "transition zone" to the emotional appeal, where qualitative reasoning becomes just as important as (if not more so than) quantitative reasoning.

## QUALITATIVE REASONING

Will the organization establish higher morale? Will communication be enhanced and problems more easily solved? Will silos disappear or at least be altered? Will the organization's image or brand be enhanced?

Qualitative reasoning is much harder to measure and report, but it's worth the effort. With a bit of cognitive effort, practically any element of qualitative reasoning can be constructed to present meaningful numeric data, two most common being customer and employee satisfaction indexes.

Every organization—public and private, large and small, product- or service-oriented—seeks the following if it is of sound business mental health:

- Sustained high morale

- Efficient and effective teamwork

- Rapid and accurate problem solving

- Positive repute and community "citizenship"

- Decreased distraction and disruption

- Accurate and unbiased communication

These "emotional" factors (sometimes referred to as "soft factors") are usually the most important when it comes to presenting your case and persuading your target. Because, as you already know, logic makes you think and emotion makes you act. All the new plant cost calculations in the world are useless unless current customers are providing the repeat business and referral business to drive the expansion. Thus, your emotional appeals should deliberately and fastidiously involve soft factors, without exception. (I've seen million-dollar construction vehicles, capable of traveling at speeds up to 1.5 miles per hour, with rounded and streamlined sides. Why? Aesthetic appeal, of course!)

Determine which emotional factors best appeal to the *other person*. Don't attempt to please yourself or choose to fulfill yourself and your needs, quantitatively and qualitatively. Rather, ensure that you address the other person's emotional needs and push the appropriate visceral hot buttons. This is not manipulative; it is the essence of sales and persuasion.

### Measuring the Unmeasurable

"You can't measure morale!" some shout. "You can't measure enthusiasm!" Okay, fair enough, but that doesn't mean we shouldn't try. I have a two-step method to help prove the unprovable. First, describe an observable behavior that you believe is an indicator of the desired result. Second, count the occurrences. If you're seeking sustained high morale, perhaps you note whether people are on time for staff meetings, or perhaps you calculate what percentage of the staff is displaying positive emotions during a meeting. If you're seeking efficient and effective teamwork, you count the number of times people come into your office asking for you to settle disputes. If you're trying to build positive repute, you could count positive media mentions.

Is this a perfect method? Of course not, but it is certainly better and more accurate than using intuition alone. And, when you attach measures to the qualitative reasoning of your case, many will find it more compelling.

## Emotion Basics

To be compelling, you need to conjure emotions within your target. More than 400 words exist in the English language to describe the concept of "emotion." In fact, neurologists have even identified distinctions between emotions (the automatic brain response) and feelings (the subjective way we interpret those emotions). Depending on how thinly you'd like to slice the topic, you could literally list dozens of human emotions, probably right off the top of your head—from acceptance, affection, and aggression to pity, pleasure, and pride, to shame, suffering, and sympathy. And of course, there are various levels of intensity of any particular emotion.

To simplify things, let's just consider for the moment that there are three categories of emotions: positive, neutral, and negative. Below are some descriptors of several emotional variations in each category.

| Positive | Neutral | Negative |
|----------|---------|----------|
| Affection | Acceptance | Aggression |
| Compassion | Disinterest | Hostility |
| Contentment | Distraction | Boredom |
| Gratitude | Indifference | Regret |
| Hope | Realism | Despair |

When we have language, as above, to describe emotions, we are better able to specifically recognize them in ourselves and others, and to work to create those particular emotions. This begs the question: Do we ever want to create negative emotions? Well, in a word, yes.

### The Power of Negative Emotions

Obviously, many times you seek to create positive emotions in your target: If you want to be hired for the job, you'd like the person in charge of hiring to have interest in and believe in you and your abilities. If you're looking to partner with a venture capitalist, you'd want your potential partner to be ecstatic about your idea. These examples are self-evident, but there also may be times when you need to provoke a negative emotion. For example, when attempting to convince a sluggish manager that it's finally time to do something about his department's lackluster customer service, make him feel the same frustration you, your colleagues, and your clients feel about his insufficiencies in that area. You may even want him to experience some regret, as he realizes he's not reaching his full potential as a department head.

If you induce someone to temporarily experience a negative emotion (with the aim that it becomes the catalyst for that person to fix a problem), is that, in itself, a problem? Well, no. Beware, however, that—just like rafting through grade five white water—it's the way in which you navigate the rapids that determines your success.

One final note about negative emotions: We've all heard that emotions are infectious. "Enthusiasm is contagious!" is an oft-cited notion.

Well, the research is in. Scientists now say that negative emotions are actually more contagious than positive ones. So induce them judiciously!

## Emotional Objectives

It's time to get strategic and purposeful about how you plan on using emotions on your journey to yes. What emotions *could* you create? What emotions *should* you create, so that you can do the right thing for all involved? Here are seven emotional objectives to consider when building your case to persuade or dissuade.

1. *Provoke*, by causing a reaction, especially an angry one.

2. *Inspire*, by giving people hope or a reason to agree with you.

3. *Invoke*, by enabling someone to see a particular image in his or her mind.

4. *Awaken*, by making someone experience a new feeling or emotion.

5. *Arouse*, by exciting someone with ideas or possibilities.

6. *Touch*, by generating a sad or sympathetic emotion.

7. *Ignite*, by invoking a feeling of success or accomplishment.

Building one or more of these emotional strategies into your business case will materially improve your chances of yes success.

## The Physical Impact of Emotions

Emotions have been studied in almost every way imaginable. Scientists have scrupulously examined and interpreted voice-pitch characteristics, facial expressions, color choices, and so forth. Biological testing of the brain, fingertips, and saliva proves that as emotions measurably change, so does that individual's physiology. In one United Kingdom study reported by the *Washington Times* in 2008, test subjects, particularly women, experienced an increase of testosterone in their saliva after being exposed to high-performance sports-car racing.

You're probably not comfortable asking your coworkers to slide into an MRI machine or requesting permission to swab a client's tongue, but there are still several ways to measure the emotional appeal of your case. They are the very same qualitative measures that we discussed earlier in this chapter.

### Synthesizing Quantitative and Qualitative Justifications

Scenarios constantly shift along the corporate landscape, thanks to the vagaries of competitive action, government regulation, demographic change, globalization, and technological improvements (and obsolescence). Those individuals and organizations solely focused on quantitative arguments undermine qualitative arguments. But fear not; the emotional pull will prevail—even though it might involve taking a risk.

Risk involves ample degrees of probability and seriousness. Probability simply means *how likely* an event is to occur. Seriousness means *how detrimental* it will be to your situation if it does. By using these two simple, yet powerful, indexes, you can reduce the perceived risk and sometimes completely vitiate it. "Risk" as a concept can be deafening, but probability and seriousness—two quantitative tools you can bring to bear—often reduce the roar to mere background sounds.

For example, you may favor the recall of a product your customers are complaining about. However, you also might meet resistance among colleagues who claim that a recall announcement on one product would cause customers to request refunds for or fixes to other products—even though there is nothing wrong with those products. It is a dilemma, for sure, but you will win the day if you point out that the probability of more people wanting a replacement of the product in question is high, and furthermore that the seriousness of this approach is low, because there are ample stockpiles of the product, shipping can be done in bulk, and the company has sufficient cash reserves to support the proactive gesture. With no recall, however, the probability is high that adverse stories about the product in the media could affect sales of your company's other goods, the federal government might launch an investigation, and lawsuits (both individual and class action) would be filed.

Consider the plight of automaker GM, under investigation in 2014 by the U.S. House Energy and Commerce Committee for taking more than a decade to recall 2.6 million vehicles with a defective ignition switch that allowed the car to shut off while being driven. The case propelled GM into a public relations nightmare, with company CEO Mary Barra testifying in very public appearances on Capitol Hill. You wouldn't want to be in *her* shoes! Similarly, the degree of seriousness if your company chose not to recall the faulty product could include a monumental financial burden, the undermining of future product launches, and destruction of company credibility with investors.

Once again, you can see the synergies between quantitative and qualitative justification. The key: Use the power of emotion to grab attention for your argument; then augment your position with a logical case that will reassure doubters.

### Building a Bulletproof Argument

Ultimately, we're talking about creating both real and hypothetical case studies to prove a point. (Lawyers regularly do this, defending clients with "hypotheticals" to test the response of the prosecution.) To best convince others that your emotional case is relevant and powerful, consider these techniques:

- *Draw from other industries* by demonstrating how and when your idea has worked elsewhere and why it's likely to work here. Show precedent (another thing that the law relies on heavily).

- *Leverage contemporary issues.* For example, you can suggest that the hoopla and distraction of Y2K was completely unwarranted, or that the creation of a strategic petroleum reserve was an act of sheer genius. What other contemporary issues can help you state your case?

- *Provide examples* that support why quick action is necessary or a more measured approach is appropriate. Remember "Weapons of Mass Destruction" and the war that resulted?

- *Create "positional critical mass."* In other words, focus your early arguments on the movers and shakers, champions and avatars, who can best rally support for your position. It also helps when formal (hierarchical) and informal individuals (popular colleagues) support the position you espouse.

- *Cite external experts* (living and deceased) who can be leveraged to help cut through uncertainty. If I were attempting to persuade about technology, I'd cite Walt Mossberg, former *Wall Street Journal* columnist and creator of the popular conference D: All Things Digital; if my persuasion priority involved organizational strategy, I'd reference the late management consultant Peter Drucker.

- *Provide opportunities for validation and verification.* Present the metrics (quantitative help, once again) that will justify and validate your persuasion priority. For example, if you have 20 percent more clients six months from now than you do today, you'll know your organization's referral initiative will have been successful.

- *Argue against yourself.* People routinely write books that span both sides of an issue. Academic debating requires the ability to take either side of an issue and prove or disprove it. Make the anticipated arguments against your own case and rebut them, so that you're prepared for the crucible. (In the law, this is called a "mock court.")

One of the reasons I've deliberately used legal comparisons in this chapter on quantitative and qualitative reasoning, logic and emotion, is that the law is generally considered to be black and white. In reality, it consists of varying *shades of gray*. If that weren't the case, why would we need judges and juries?

Every persuasive argument contains both quantitative and qualitative aspects. Not only can't you afford to omit either dynamic, but you must appreciate the supporting role each plays for the other, as I've attempted to depict here. Mastering a synthesis of the two components will place you far ahead of the other persuaders—both those at the table *and* those down the block.

## TARGET INTELLIGENCE

Now that you have a clearer sense for how you're going to articulate your argument, let's briefly return to the topic first introduced in Chapter 3—namely, your specific target. The primary rule of communication is "know your audience." To maximize the chances that your persuasive efforts will be successful, you need not only to have an airtight pitch, but also to know key facts about the person to whom you're pitching it.

### What You Need to Know

There are three key categories to explore: personal information, preferences, and parameters. You won't need to provide every detail for each category, but the more information you have, the better your chances of persuasion success will be. You'll also be amazed at what you'll learn.

So let's begin: What do you know about your target?

### Personal Information

- *Professional objectives:* These goals are important to a person's business or career, which may involve status in a hierarchical structure, entrepreneurialism, or business ownership.

- *Personal agendas:* These goals involve family, friends, hobbies, travel, recreation, civic and service involvement, religious commitments, and self-development.

- *Emotional intensity:* This comes into play if a persuasion situation also involves a personal relationship, a belief that goes beyond intellectual evaluations, or commitment over compliance. Think of emotional intensity as the volume knob on a Marshall half stack, not the on/off switch. You can turn it up or down, depending on your needs.

- *Personality considerations:* Is there a style clash between your personality and that of your target? Is his Driving, Expressive, Amiable, or Analytical tendency (see page 49) blocking your efforts?

- *Gender or generational differences:* Are you two potentially out of sync because of behavior tendencies influenced by gender? Are generational differences creating a stone wall between you?

- *Organizational influence:* What is your target's organizational horsepower?

- *Publicly stated perspective on a given issue:* This can include conversations, written communication, the championing of or opposition to similar issues, role as a stakeholder, and experience with the given situation.

- *Trust level:* What is the degree of trust shared between you and your target? Think of your personal history with the target, respect given and shown, mutual obligations, favors supplied, and reciprocal support.

**Preferences**

- *Communication:* Does your target prefer to communicate with you and others via email, phone, or text message?

- *Data:* Some people want all the information; others just want the executive summary. Some people like to study the stats; others like to hear the story. How does your target prefer her information?

- *Work:* Does he approach problem solving in a particular way? Does she have a go-to person? Does he often resort to cutting expenses or sales promotions? Does she exhibit behaviors that may impede your path to yes?

- *Interpersonal:* Examine your target's advisers, peers, and sources of influence. Does your target have any exceptionally positive or unusually strained relationships? Also evaluate the probability of whether she will act independently or succumb to peer pressure.

**Parameters**

- *Approval authority:* This usually relates to economics, budgets, and the ability to secure funding by attracting donors or underwriters. (Note: Knowing this detail is crucial when dealing with targets in nonprofit organizations.)

- *Budget jurisdiction:* This relates to your target's ability to make unilateral decisions, control timing in the budget process, determine ROI considerations, change priorities, and allocate discretionary funds.

- *Time constraints:* Consider the deadlines you and your target are under, the magnitude of what needs to be accomplished once agreement is reached, and the hours/days/months/years it will take to make the concept of the ask a reality.

- *Issue expertise:* This may involve credibility, history in this and similar circumstances, ability to research and study the issue, and public statements.

You may wish to add or amend categories. My point is that in order to define your target *and the likelihood of persuasion*, you need intelligence—not brain smarts, but what the government would call "intel." I choose not to think of this as "competitive intelligence," because the target isn't necessarily in a competitive position (at least we should hope not). But the target is in a questionable position, insofar as how amenable that individual might be to your persuasive charms.

As humans, we rely on hearsay, body language, or visceral reaction for information. However, keep in mind that perception biases can mislead you. You're better off beginning with a *tabula rasa*, or a blank slate, which you can fill with logical answers to intelligent questions in relevant categories. Don't guess or simply rely on what you've always believed. Often, what you've perceived about others is not accurate and is sometimes antithetical to a particular person's actual positions.

### How to Get the Intel

It's easy to say *what* to do, but the larger question is how to do it. Here are seven ways to gather evidence:

1. *Be present.* When you're attending meetings, working with others, or engaging in "hall chat," try not to be consumed with your own tasks and agenda. These are key times to discover crucial clues that can help you find yes more often.

2. *Learn to watch and listen.* What someone says and how that person says it can tell you a lot. You know your target's hierarchical rank, but how carefully are you really listening to him? Pay attention to the inflection, tone, and degree of passion with which your target is communicating. How close is he already to your position on the issue? Be alert to the reality of the moment.

3. *Review applicable internal and external information.* Think about the conventions, beliefs, protocols, and values people employ to govern their actions. Have conversations, not interrogations. Subtlety is an art form: Rather than say, "What do you know about the organizational politics regarding this project in marketing?" try, "Do you think the new project will be a tough sell to marketing?"

4. *Use the FORM model for conversations.* In other words, bring up "Family," "Occupation," "Recreation," and "Motivation" in con-

versations with your target. ("Tell me about your *family*. What do you like best about your *occupation*? What do you do for *recreation*? What's your *motivation* for working on this project?")

5. *Master the fine art of secret polling.* Once people make their opinions known, they are loath to change them. That's why it's far easier to change the mind of someone who hasn't yet made a public statement. In jury deliberations, a foreperson sometimes asks fellow jurors to state guilty or not guilty verdicts anonymously on pieces of paper; this is known as "secret polling," and it is an effective way of revealing early opinions without forcing anyone to make a public commitment. The takeaway: Attempt to find positions privately without demanding, or even innocently inducing, a public declaration.

6. *Practice convergent validity.* Don't believe anything until you've obtained three pieces of evidence to support it. The following Sufi parable will help put this action into context: *Three blind wanderers encountered an elephant in the jungle. "What have we here?" they exclaimed together. The first man, standing alongside the great beast, said, "It's like a wall." The second, who was holding one of the legs, replied, "No, it's like a tree trunk." And the third, tangling with the trunk, said, "I don't know what you two are talking about, but this thing is like a snake."* Bridging all three perspectives brings the wanderers (and you) closer to the truth.

7. *Use the "nod quad."* The following four questions help you hear yes in almost any evidence-gathering situation, so I call them the "nod quad." You won't always use all of them, or use them in any particular sequence, but put these in your pocket and pull them out, as needed, to help you find the information you need:

    1. How much organizational agreement is there about the challenges we're facing as a company?

2. When you say _____ (time, money, risk, resistance), what specifically do you mean?

3. What are you most excited about in your world right now?

4. Do you think _____ (this proposal, this initiative, this idea) will be a tough sell in _____ (marketing, legal, research)?

The more significant your request, the more careful your intel gathering should be. When it comes to major projects, issues near and dear to your value system, and asks important to your career, you can't afford to do anything less than engage in some serious quantitative and qualitative reasoning. People who are "natural" persuaders already go through this kind of process automatically and viscerally, without much conscious effort. Call it "unconscious competency." You can get there, too.

---

### Chapter 4 Persuasion Points

1. Recognize that quantitative factors are often the default factors in a persuasive situation.

2. Master the fundamental business measures and calculations that most frequently arise in meetings and discussions.

3. Acquire assistance, if necessary, in arcane financial issues so that you can discuss them authoritatively.

4. Be aware that, while logic prompts thinking, emotion propels acting.

5. Learn to establish visceral, compelling arguments as they relate to important company considerations.

6. Use quantitative facts to provide boundaries and understanding for "softer" issues and initiatives.

7. Focus on the influencing power of risk. Articulate risk according to probability and seriousness, both for your position and the opposition's, and ensure that yours is "safer."

8. Always focus on your target's self-interests and emotional needs; that way, he will always perceive the advantage to be his.

9. Remember that gathering data about your target is an essential step in achieving your persuasive priority.

# The Credibility Crucible

**How You Get It, Why You Lose It, and
How You Win It Back**

Regardless of what line of business you're in, every organization, every department, every team has at least one person whom *everybody* trusts. When that person takes on a project, it's done well, on time, and on budget. He gives you advice? It's solid. She provides data? It's accurate. These are the people who get things done. And these are the people who hear yes more often.

In short, they possess the secret to persuasion success: killer credibility. The dictionary defines *credibility* as "the quality of being convincing or believable." I define it with one word: *essential*. Throughout your career, your credibility will be tested. All the time.

Easy to lose and tough to build, credibility ranks as one of the primary characteristics of a successful and professional persuader. A basic determination of credibility can be found in the following descriptors:

- You do what you say you're going to do.

- Your information is accurate and unbiased.

- You're not prone to exaggeration or hyperbole.

- You admit when you're wrong and accept blame.

- You share the credit when successful.

- Your word is your bond.

The key question is this: What do people say about you when you're not in the room?

## ASSESSING YOUR CREDIBILITY

Let's consider two levels, or planes, on which your persuasion credibility operates. The first plane: You have either high credibility or low credibility. Easy enough. But keep in mind that there's a difference between an event and a trend. Something that happens once is an event; three times is a trend. One success doesn't make you a rock star, and one mistake doesn't make you a failure. It's the body of work that counts.

The second plane: Are you—your skills, your abilities, and your results—*personally* known by your target? If you've worked with your target, you're known. Simple as that. If he sees you in the hallway and can call you by name, you're known. If you haven't worked with your target in the past, you're unknown. She may know *of* you, but that doesn't count.

The credibility quadrants shown in Figure 5-1 will enable you to consider which quadrant you might fall into with a particular target, and what action needs to be taken as a result.

### Known Reputation/Low Credibility

Here you have to repair your reputation, for whatever reason (and it could be situations outside your control). Start small. Make the call. Apologize. And from that point forward, promise yourself that you won't let this particular mistake happen again. Everybody makes mistakes. High earners learn from them.

**Figure 5-1**  Credibility Quadrants

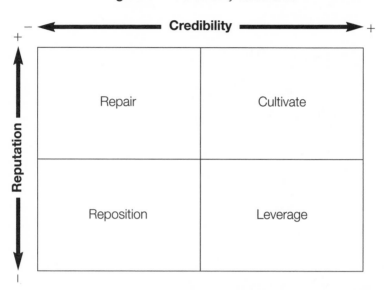

Here's an example: When the on-demand streaming and DVD-by-mail service Netflix announced a split in 2011, with the DVD piece of its business relaunching as Qwikster, customers went nuts; they were furious with the move, which came on the heels of a price increase. Netflix CEO Reed Hastings took to Netflix's blog. "I messed up," he wrote. "I owe everyone an explanation." Less than a month later, he blogged again, announcing the quick end of Qwikster. Today, Netflix has more than 44 million subscribers—proving that customers (and coworkers) are usually a pretty understanding bunch if you keep them in the loop.

If you're in a comparable predicament and you fail to act as Hastings did, you risk having others see you as disingenuous or dishonest. Here are other ways to remedy a similar situation:

- *Acknowledge prior setbacks.* Don't pretend defeats were victories and luck was talent.

- *Accept responsibility.* Share credit but corner the market on blame.

- *Request guidance.* Openly reach out for ideas and courses of action that restore credibility.

### Unknown Reputation/Low Credibility

Sometimes a bad reputation precedes you. And, not infrequently, it's the result of guilt by association. Perhaps you work in the human resources department, and in your organization, HR doesn't have the most upstanding reputation. So you're already down a notch before you enter a room.

In that case, it's essential to reposition yourself. Don't be defensive. Don't have a chip on your shoulder. Don't look for a fight. Instead, use facts, stats, and evidence to the contrary to show why the bad rap on your department might not be accurate. Here are some ways to do that:

- *Use third-party information* to help others understand the situations that created the negative impression.

- *Make reasonable, verifiable statements* about your background and intent. Put people at ease with facts.

- *Determine your target's values,* as well as his personality traits and how he processes information. Cater your strategies, conversations, and behavior appropriately.

Rarely do people have Paul-on-the-road-to-Damascus epiphanies, but as you present your target with evidence that counters the original, less-than-optimal impression, you will start to reshape, reframe, and reposition your reputation.

### Unknown Reputation/High Credibility

You and your abilities might be unknown, but you still pack high credibility, either by significant word of mouth about you or by your connection to a successful initiative. Well done. You have successfully built a reputation of being knowledgeable and dependable. So now what?

Leverage your position! Your perceived value—your "stock price," as it were—will never be higher. Here are ways to make your influence work for you:

- *Use this position to attain additional success.* Build on what you've achieved by going after more projects, more clients, and more opportunities to hear yes.

- *Negotiate terms for future deals that work to your advantage.* Take into consideration the accountabilities, the workload, the time frames, and, most important, the price. You may never be in this position again!

- *Make sure that you deliver on your newly made promises.* This brings us to our fourth, and final, quadrant.

## Known Reputation/High Credibility

If people know you, have worked with you, and think highly of you and your abilities, congratulations! You've arrived at the mountaintop. This is where people strive to be—and now it is up to you to cultivate this position.

Being in this quadrant means that people trust your input and your performance so much that they ask for and heed your advice wholeheartedly. Steve Jobs had that kind of pull. He created a demographic of computer consumers who wait in half-mile-long lines for an entire day to purchase a product they've never touched or even seen up close—all because it has the Apple logo on it.

But beware: Customer and colleague relationships are precious and should never be taken advantage of by abusing credibility to sell unnecessary, unwanted, or low-quality items. Remember Apple's short-lived MobileMe subscription service? That was a disaster, and Jobs had the integrity to admit it. And, as with Netflix's Hastings, customers forgave him. The best ways to capitalize on this quadrant are to:

- *Ensure that your actions match your reputation.* Don't allow for cognitive dissonance. Be consistent.

- *Utilize the trust that is automatically bestowed.*

- *Be mindful of your actual performance.* You can easily lose the lofty perch because you're so visible and observed.

- *Be assertive but not arrogant.* Make achievements visible but not obnoxious. You can afford to be modest.

- *Set reasonable expectations for the future.* You want a solid foundation that you can build upon, not a house of cards.

- *Be sensitive to differing perspectives* and people assessing your accomplishments through their own lenses.

Know your quadrants, and develop the skills and strategies required to work your way toward being a highly credible, known force. Credibility is *that* important.


## THREE COMPONENTS OF CREDIBILITY

Credibility cannot be achieved if you don't possess the following three attributes: expertise, track record, and respect. You can get by with two of those three, but it's going to be tough. So go for the hat trick.


### Expertise

Expertise means that you actually comport yourself as an expert. Experts' opinions are believed and sought; they are not generally subject to quibbles or arguments. No one ever walked up to Peter Drucker and challenged his thinking about management strategy.

You gain expertise through experiences, education, observations, and boldly moving on from both your victories and your defeats. It's fine to be defeated in a good cause if you learn from it. After all, you hone your skills through continual, real-world application. It's often said that saints engage in introspection, while sinners run the world. Think about that.

In today's world, which is rapidly changing through globalization and our ever-intensifying use of technology, expertise necessitates engaging in an ongoing quest, not maintaining a static position. How do you know you're an "expert"? Because people cite you, quote you, defer to you, ask your opinion, and use you as the standard—even if all that happens only within your own organization.

### Track Record

Nothing succeeds in promoting credibility like results that others can see, touch, feel, hear, and smell. In other words, don't just talk the talk; walk the walk. Track records don't require uniform and unblemished successes. In fact, showing variation is preferable. The idea is to constantly improve. The best batters in baseball, on average, get a hit only once in every three at bats.

The key idea regarding looking back on your successes and failures is to build on your strengths. We spend too much time evaluating defeats (performing postmortems) and correcting weaknesses. Determine how and why you were successful, and seek to replicate that success. If you do, weaknesses will naturally atrophy. By the way, if you look at my suggestions for each of the quadrants above, you'll note that acknowledging your "defeats" is an integral part of building your credibility.

### Respect

By "respect," I mean not merely affection. No one respects people who can win only if someone else loses, or who see life as a zero-sum game. You don't have to like everyone, but you do have to remain civil. When you share, you gain respect; you also gain respect when you accept responsibility, when you volunteer, and when you effectively negotiate and honestly resolve conflict. Engendering respect requires the savvy use of interpersonal skills. The ways in which you communicate with colleagues, associates, and clients play a large role in credibility and prove your ability (or inability) to create allies instead of adversaries.

An important factor in leveraging these three components is your willingness to coach others. Coaching builds your expertise, your track record, and your respect. It's like "one-stop shopping." As Yogi Bhajan, the late spiritual leader and entrepreneur who introduced kundalini yoga to the United States, once said: "If you want to learn something, read about it. If you want to understand something, write about it. If you want to master something, teach it."

## ACQUIRING, LOSING, AND REBUILDING CREDIBILITY

Once you've established credibility, there's no guarantee you'll hold on to it forever. Circumstances beyond your control (or of your own doing) can cause you to lose a little or a lot of credibility. When that happens, you must find a way to recoup those losses and come back stronger than ever. In this section, we'll demonstrate behaviors that lead to various outcomes.

### Four Ways to Build Credibility

Gaining credibility is easier than you might think. In fact, you might already have established a significant degree of credibility among your professional peers and not even know it. If you currently do any of the following, you're well on your way to creating credibility confidence.

- *Publicize your successes.* Demonstrate your triumphs, relate your victories, recount your progresses—but don't boast about them. And just because a success may be small doesn't mean it isn't worth noting or discussing. Nothing breeds like success—and it is more likely to breed if people know about it.

- *Create a "rational future."* In other words, help people see a future that begins pragmatically in the present and develops logically and persuasively forward along a reasonable path. I observed Steve Ballmer in 2000 (after he succeeded Bill Gates as CEO) attempt to rally the troops at Microsoft's 25th anniversary bash, and what he intended as a show of great energy and passion came across as almost berserk ravings (which is exactly what the press reported and the investors perceived). Ballmer retired from the company in early 2014 after 14 years at the helm.

- *Become clearly accessible and accountable—or, to use contemporary jargon, "transparent."* I remember some college professors who held regular office hours and seemed genuinely happy to welcome students, and others who seemed to take wicked pleasure in ignoring their students. The former had far more credibility among students when it came to their opinions and critiques. After all, people are less likely to argue with an individual who is clearly available and responsible.

- *Hang out with other credibility all-stars.* Leadership coach Marshall Goldsmith says that in order to be a thought leader, you must surround yourself with other thought leaders. The same principle applies to credibility. Find people with impressive credibility credentials within your organization or community and align yourself with them. Learn from them and support them, and eventually you'll become like them.

## Four Ways to Lose Credibility

Only one condition is worse than not having credibility—having had credibility and losing it. Credibility lost is extremely hard to regain, so let's look at the causes (with an eye toward preventing this from happening).

- *Stop succeeding.* If your success track record ends, so will your credibility. Either you will fail to make continuous progress and achieve victories, or you will continue to do so but no one will know.

- *Deceive people.* Most unethical conduct in corporations is committed for the organization's gain, not one's personal gain. But that doesn't lessen the impact. "White lies" in business—unlike those in family situations, where the complete truth might significantly hurt a loved one—can be tolerated in very few situations. When someone knows that you've lied, that person immediately wonders what else you've been (or are or will be) lying about. And *that*, friends, throws your credibility over the edge of the cliff.

- *Fail to share credit.* That's why I continue to emphasize accepting blame and sharing credit. It's better to risk providing credit to even peripheral contributors than to fail to reward even one person.

- *Allow your ego to become the size of a balloon in the Macy's Thanksgiving Day Parade.* If you think only of, about, and for yourself, that will become quickly apparent to those around you. You must demonstrate that you're acting with others in mind via gestures of generosity that are clearly visible. A simple and public "thank you" often packs more punch than a reward handed over in the privacy of an office. There are reasons why the U.S. military puts medals on people in front of a lot of other people.

Can you return from credibility self-immolation? It's tough, but yes. And when you do, you'll be joining a club of famous people who came back from the abyss to reinvent their careers (and, in some cases, attain even higher heights), including Bill Clinton, Hugh Grant, Robert McNamara, Tiger Woods, and Jack Welch.

### Ten Steps to Win Back Credibility

As chairman and CEO at General Electric for 20 years between 1981 and 2001, Jack Welch became known as "Neutron Jack," because his often-draconian decisions eliminated people while leaving buildings unscathed. However, when GE suffered a variety of public bruisings—scandals within the multinational corporation's credit department that involved price-fixing with diamonds in South Africa and money-laundering and fraud in Israel—Welch unilaterally announced that henceforward managers were required not only to meet performance goals, but to do so within the company's value system. Doing one or the other would be insufficient. In short order, a conglomerate that manufactured everything from lightbulbs to locomotives became a model company because Jack Welch had regained his, and his company's, credibility.

Hugh Grant, after being caught with a prostitute in Los Angeles two weeks before the 1995 release of his first major studio film, *Nine Months*, regained credibility by following a totally different path: He went on *The Tonight Show* with Jay Leno, whereupon the host famously asked him, "What the hell were you thinking?" Grant's response: "I think you know in life what's a good thing to do and what's a bad thing, and I did a bad thing. And there you have it." He went on to become a successful leading man in Hollywood—in part, I'll argue, because he admitted his mistake and blamed no one but himself. That's one way to mend a credibility gap.

President Bill Clinton, another man whose moral temptations got the best of him, was impeached for his actions related to his inappropriate relationship with an intern and later for lying to Congress about his behavior. Today, he's regarded as a consensus builder and a brilliant politician. Likewise, a great many people are once again cheering for Tiger Woods on every tee and green. So don't feel as though you cannot regain trust and credibility. Here are 10 steps to put you back in good grace with colleagues and associates:

*Step 1: Assess the damage.* Try to understand what really occurred, factually and perceptively, that caused you to lose credibility. If you need objective help, don't be afraid to ask others, because you can't afford to underestimate the damage or assume it will pass with time. The damage O. J. Simpson did to his credibility did *not* pass with time.

*Step 2: Admit your error.* Honesty counts for a whole lot in business. As stated earlier, lies have no place in running an ethical operation. Lying about a mistake or passing the blame will only undo whatever credibility you've managed to hold on to.

*Step 3: Learn the language of apology.* As Netflix's Hastings discovered, admitting a mistake or wrongdoing may not be enough. You need to understand the power of apologetic language. Sharing information about pending and completed decisions, apologizing for mistakes, and listening to and responding to concerns, questions, and comments are at the core of leadership credibility.

*Step 4: Start rebuilding credibility with small steps.* Engage a few people or groups at a time, focusing on low-key topics and noncontroversial issues. Make sure you deliver what you promise when you promise.

*Step 5: Channel your inner Johnny Carson.* Johnny Carson is one of my all-time favorite American entertainers. One of the best. When a guest would mention a current event or piece of knowledge outside Johnny's realm, the host didn't feign understanding, try to take over the conversation, or "one up" the guest. He simply said, "I did not know that." That's what I say now, and you should, too.

*Step 6: Realize that credibility is a volume knob, not an on/off switch.* It's impossible to be "mostly pregnant," but you can be "mostly credible." Seek success, not perfection. Think of the needle registering on a gauge: You want it to keep rising, which represents strong and steady progress. It doesn't need to be revving on the red line to be working properly.

*Step 7: Remember that all things are relative.* Nobody is asking you to be "the most credible" person ever at your job. You simply need to be credible. It doesn't matter if you're the most popular guy in the office or the best-liked gal in your department; so why strive to be the most credible? Such distinctions carry very little weight in most cases.

*Step 8: Conduct conversations about your lapse.* This will allow you to prove you're in a better place now. Just don't raise the issue incessantly. If you're comfortable conversing about it, you're going to make it a topic of conversation and not a cause célèbre.

*Step 9: Allow some events to fade, especially if they're minor.* Don't keep reminding people of every previous transgression. You may have been tipsy at an office party, but someone else probably drank a lot more.

*Step 10: Shake it off.* Don't let mistakes undermine everything you do. Ignore the "doom loop" mentality of struggling with a credibility issue or an incident that serves only to further undermine your confidence and credibility. Let it go the way an athlete overcomes a minor injury. Don't go running to the training room or, worse, admit yourself to the hospital.

### How Don Imus Reengineered His Credibility

Don Imus has been a syndicated radio talk show host for more than three decades, the winner of four Marconi Awards, and a well-known media personality who always seemed to wear his signature cowboy hat. His show (also broadcast on TV in many markets) is irreverent, sarcastic, and ironic, while also being provocative and featuring members of Congress, famous authors, scientists, and celebrities.

In 2007, Imus and his producer, during the course of on-air banter, made incredibly inappropriate and racist remarks about the Rutgers University women's basketball team. Reaction was swift and decisive. Imus was suspended, then fired—a 40-year career gone after 40 seconds of thoughtless, offensive comments. Even many of his stalwart supporters in the media failed to have his back.

What did Imus do with his newfound free time? He went on the apology circuit, embracing the media and even appearing on Al Sharpton's radio show in New York, where he knew he'd be pummeled. He visited the Rutgers women's basketball team. After six months, he returned to the airwaves with a larger syndicated network and achieved higher ratings than ever. Today, Imus is back on top.

Sometimes he discusses his humongous error in judgment and expresses how much he regrets it. This makes Imus an excellent example of credibility rehabilitation.

## THE BOTTOM LINE ON CREDIBILITY

Is credibility the shield to prevent bad things from ever happening to you? Of course not. We live in a what-have-you-done-for-me-lately world. An interviewer once asked Jerry Seinfeld if his television success had any positive impact on his stand-up act. "Yes, it buys me about five minutes," the comedian replied. "After that, I'd better be funny."

Same thing applies here. If you are perceived as being a credible individual, you get about a five-minute leeway. After that, you'd better be credible. Period.

---

### Chapter 5 Persuasion Points

1. Credibility is in the eye of the beholder; look through the other person's lens.

2. You can have high credibility, even as an "unknown."

3. Focus on expertise, track record, and respect.

4. You can consciously build and nurture credibility.

5. You also can recapture and rehabilitate credibility.

6. Don't seek perfection; seek progress.

7. Some memories fade, which you should allow.

8. Don't make a bad situation worse by overthinking it.

9. If Bill Clinton and Hugh Grant can rehabilitate their credibility, so can you.

# Power Language

**Verbal and Nonverbal Communication
Tools to Skyrocket Your Success**

Every year around the holiday season, I like to buy books for family and friends. Independent and chain stores alike tend to have a small display behind the checkout counter featuring a colorful arrangement of classic children's books—usually ones, such as *The Berenstain Bears*, that I remember reading or having read to me. Inevitably, the bookseller at the register will ask me some variation of this question: "We're collecting new-book donations for the city's childhood literacy programs. A single book can be used to teach hundreds of kids to read. Can you help by donating one?"

Who *wouldn't* want to help kids learn to read? For a moment, I think back to the days when I knew all the names of the Berenstain Bears, and then I realize that I'd like to help other kids learn their names, too. "Sure," I told the clerk last time this happened, spotting the book on display I wanted to donate. "I'd like to give a copy of *The Berenstain Bears Show Some Respect*." Not only did I perform a good deed, I was swayed by her rhetoric—that is, the art of persuasive speaking or writing. The clerk's sales pitch, designed to appeal to my emotions and my generous book-buying mood, motivated me to say yes.

The connotations of *rhetoric* have changed in recent years to suggest that it is a pejorative form of discourse, as in, "empty political rhetoric." But the original definition is "the art of persuasive speaking and writing, especially using figures of speech." It's about the entirety of your communication. Effective rhetoric involves verbal and nonverbal communication skills, which in turn dictate how persuasive you are by informing others of your intent—overtly and covertly, explicitly and implicitly.

## LANGUAGE MISPERCEPTIONS

Contrary to popular belief, the word *verbal* does not mean "spoken"; rather, it means "utilizing words." *What* you say and *how* you say it are often equally important. I'm going to repeat that—*equally important*. Let's call it the "steak" (content) and the "sizzle" (delivery). Professional speakers—at least the good ones—learn quickly that their delivery will determine the degree to which the audience will pay attention, especially at the outset of their talk.

Albert Mehrabian, professor emeritus of psychology at UCLA, is often misquoted in the area of language research. While it's true he tested the effects of such social interactions as cutting into a crowded line and determining whether a smile and/or a quick excuse would lead to greater acceptance of the transgression (both did), Mehrabian's research became distorted over the years. It's now characterized as proving that words simply don't matter. Some of the misinformed even go as far as to use a fictitious statistic that suggests words are only 4 percent of the power of communication, with style counting for 96 percent.

That's nonsense, and you know it.

An example of how words still matter can be found in a *Wall Street Journal* evaluation of real estate ads and their language effectiveness. When the ads mentioned "handyman's special," those homes sold at a 50 percent faster rate than average—and at a 30 percent lower price! Those ads that stated the home was in "move-in condition" sold 12 percent faster, "starter home" listings sold 9 percent faster, and those ads that described the homeowner as a "motivated seller" lowered the sale price but actually slowed the sale. When garages were mentioned, sales increased 9.8 percent; when fireplaces were included, sales climbed 6.8 percent. And if a lake was mentioned, the home sold 5.6 percent faster. Perhaps surprisingly, the words *must sell* had no impact on results.

## SAVVY WORD CHOICES

It's been said before by so many but bears repeating, especially in discussions about persuasion: Logic makes you think; emotion makes you act. Some words are more compelling than others because of their emotional heft. They create powerful mental images to which listeners can readily relate.

That's why some of the best word choices evoke aspirational, emotional, and perilous concepts. In other words, they are terms that compliment and inspire; prompt an immediate response; and spell out potential consequences or risks, respectively. Consider the following:

- Our *savviest* customers; the company's *diverse* suite of products; your *compelling* presentation.

- A *sensitive* situation; an *urgent* response; a *feel-good* solution.

- If we don't act now, we might have to *forfeit* this opportunity; are you really willing to *surrender* to the competition?

Unpack your trunk of adjectives and punch up the power quotient. Instead of just saying the team has to make a decision, try describing it as a *crucial* decision, or perhaps a *far-reaching* decision, or a *key* decision. Describe another person's perspective as *enlightened, critical,* or *well-informed.* And you'll often see these words repeatedly used in advertising copy, because they repeatedly work: *fast, easy, guaranteed, powerful, quick, inexpensive.*

Remember that a strength overdone is a weakness. Judiciously used, well-chosen adjectives can work tremendously; overuse, on the other hand, leads to hyperbole.

## Context Matters

As briefly alluded to in Chapter 5, people who believe they are receiving conflicting messages between what they hear and what they see will default to what they're seeing. This is called "cognitive dissonance." Thus, in order to achieve some profundity, you must understand and synthesize the importance and reach of both verbal and nonverbal messages. You can do so by choosing the right word for your intent *and* your audience.

Pop quiz: Do you know what these three words mean?

- Grueling

- Arduous

- Operose

They all mean essentially the same thing: "involving great labor." You might use *grueling* casually at a bar or with your kids, *arduous* could be appropriate with learned friends at a formal dinner, and *operose* may best be reserved for use in a fictional piece or an academic setting (or maybe not at all). In other words, never dumb down your language, but choose it carefully.

## Six Words That Will *Always* Make a Difference

When in the process of persuading, remember six powerful words that will force you to link a meaningful target benefit to your ask: "What this means to you is . . ." You can't say it without saying something after it, of course. So when you start to focus on your justification points for why someone should take you up on your offer, liberally use this phrase as part of your rhetoric.

Say, for example, you sell guitars and you're trying to explain to a potential customer why the Gibson line is superior to the less expensive Epiphone. "Epiphone guitars use a polyurethane finish that dries rock hard. Gibson guitars use a more expensive nitrocellulose finish that allows the wood to vibrate. *What this means to you* is that you'll have that classic Gibson tone, which is immediately recognizable and one you can't get with really any other instrument."

And what this means to *you* is . . . you'll hear yes more often.

## HOW "FIGURE SKATING" RELATES TO PERSUASION

Another way to convincingly state your case is by relying on figures of speech. I call this practice "figure skating," to emphasize that metaphor, simile, analogy, and chiasmus are significant verbal tools in your persuasion box—and that the act of using them can be elevated to an art form.

### Metaphors

A metaphor is the use of one example to mean another, one that is not literally applicable. For example, the term *escape velocity* is the speed needed to break free of the Earth's gravitational pull. Yet it also can describe the effort needed to leave behind old thinking and moribund habits: "We need to reevaluate our escape velocity." Metaphors travel in the high-speed language lane, whisking you down the road much faster than merely using plain, bumper-to-bumper words does. (See how easy this is?)

Here are some more metaphors:

- That guy is the LeBron James of R&D. Put the ball in his hands and watch what happens next.

- The proposed region is the Siberia of markets: hard to reach, excessively regulated, and plagued by both an intolerable climate and poor communication. Why do we want to go there?

- Winning that account would give us license to print our own money.

## Similes

A close cousin of the metaphor, the simile is a comparison using *like* or *as* to vividly compare two unlike things. Simile clichés include "cool as a cucumber," "smart as a fox," and "thin as a rail." Avoid the clichés and try using similes to describe outcomes that persuade listeners to become more invested in your ask:

- The potential cash flow would be like Niagara Falls.

- He would be as poorly received as Miley Cyrus opening for Metallica.

- That promotional strategy is about as elegant as a pig wearing Armani.

Similes are used frequently (and often unconsciously) to convey subliminal persuasion, because what's occurring is a subconscious agreement based on another (and often different) circumstance.

Think of the major professional or personal persuasion priorities you might face within the next three months, and then write down three relevant similes. If you want to convince your boss to boost the company website's content marketing strategy, for example, consider saying this: "To not invest in video production right now would be like hurling ourselves in a time machine back to 1999."

## Analogies

Analogies are similar to metaphors and similes but are based on more realistic comparisons rather than improbable ones (like Miley Cyrus touring with Metallica). Common analogies include "a fish out of water," "their relationship is beginning to thaw," and "quiet as a mouse."

Here are some business-applicable analogies:

- Selling our product is like playing shortstop in the Major Leagues—it looks easy until you try it.

- Entering that market would be like exploring a funhouse: Just when you think you've seen everything, the floor collapses.

- I don't understand why people go on winery tours; do you watch cows grazing in a field because you like to eat burgers?

These primary figures of speech are just the beginning to finding creative, descriptive ways to convince your target with words. Next is a lesser-known literary device that is fun to use and works like a charm.

## Chiasmi

A chiasmus is a verbal pattern in which the second half of a phrase is balanced against the first, with key elements being reversed. While you may not be familiar with the term, chances are you've encountered the format. One of the most famous came from John F. Kennedy: "Ask not what your country can do for you, ask what you can do for your country." Other renowned chiasmi? "I am stuck on Band-Aid brand 'cause Band-Aid's stuck on me!" and "StarKist doesn't want tunas with good taste. StarKist wants tunas that taste good."

Think about these types of reversals to make your points:

- Do you want your money in the bank or the bank in your money?

- Do we want to face the competition now or have the competition in our face later?

- How can marketing keep spending money if there is no money to spend?

Even "The Golden Rule" is based on a chiasmus: Treat others as you would like others to treat you. (Although we know, in terms of persuasion, it's a little off!)

Other powerful figures of speech can be used persuasively in business situations as well, including antitheses (It's never too late, and it's never too early) and paradoxes (You can save money by spending it). Figures of speech work well in persuasion because they allow you and your target to have fun with words. When that's happening, it's easier to get to yes.

**Mark's Power Play**

One powerful way of using language is to heighten the sense of risk with your target and then give your recommendation about how to proceed. My favorite way of raising risk is with a chiasmus: "It's one thing to have the insurance and not need it. It's a completely different situation to need it and not have it."

*That's* an interesting notion. Now I'm a bit more concerned. Attach that with something called "anticipated regret" and you're really getting somewhere. This is when you ask your target to consider the angst she would feel if she didn't follow your advice and made a bad decision as a result. Researchers have proved that people are much more inclined to take your advice if they first considered what might happen if they didn't. "How bad would you feel if, after we had this conversation, you found yourself in a situation where you were exposed?"

Then you need to take your flashlight and lead your target through the darkness—and make an expert recommendation. "So here's what I'm going to recommend. Get the insurance. That way, if you need it, you're covered."

## WHY STORIES WORK

Storytelling is one of the oldest, most effective forms of human communication. Long before Twitter, Facebook, and even the printing press, humans informed and instructed others via stories. The tradition probably began some 3 million years ago with members of the species

*Australopithecus africanus* making wild hand gestures while sitting around a tree. Communication then progressed to the first cave drawings, no doubt thanks to some braggart talking big about his latest saber-toothed tiger kill.

Since then, storytelling as a communication art form has stood the test of time. Why? Because it's compelling. Just try listening to only half of Jim Croce's "You Don't Mess Around with Jim," Gordon Lightfoot's "The Wreck of the *Edmund Fitzgerald*," or Harry Chapin's "Cat's in the Cradle." It's almost impossible. Even if you've heard those songs before, you still want to know how each story ends.

Stories also can be instrumental in helping you convince others—a colleague, a potential customer, or maybe even a complete stranger in an elevator. I call them "situational persuasion success stories." These are pre-created retellings of how you previously helped improve someone's condition in particular situations. This elevated skill set can yield tremendous results in your persuasion efforts and will accomplish five things. You will:

1. *Create a nonthreatening way to share information.* In many persuasion situations, your target can be on hyperalert, wanting to avoid feeling uninformed or ambushed. And if the conversation is focused on him, his personal defenses may be heightened. When you make your point with a story that does not involve the present individual, it's much easier for your target to relax and focus on the discussion. Humorous stories, especially those that are self-deprecating, can help relieve tension and create common bonds.

2. *Allow your target to insert herself into the role of your story's main character.* The best situational persuasion success stories are ones in which the main character is someone other than you or the target. Inserting yourself into the lead role could send the wrong message—suggesting that you are self-centered and your story is contrived. So don't be the hero in every story; make the main character someone else, such as a friend or colleague, to

whom your target can relate. "Been there, done that" is the best listener engagement you could ask for.

3. *Make the discussion an effective one.* Everyone enjoys a good story now and then, and situational persuasion success stories contain three subtle yet distinct objectives: to inform, educate, and persuade. When you inform someone, you make that person aware; when you educate, you bring about understanding; and when you persuade, you enable your target to embrace a particular point of view—yours.

4. *Provide a "social proof" component.* As one of my professional heroes, Robert Cialdini, author of *Influence: The Psychology of Persuasion*, claims, "We follow the lead of similar others." When we hear "all the kids are doing it," that has a profound impact on us. Using situational persuasion success stories leverages this idea of social proof, and makes what you're talking about even more convincing.

5. *Break through the surrounding informational noise.* In his book *Data Smog: Surviving the Information Glut* (San Francisco: Harper Edge), author David Shenk states that the average American in 1971 encountered 560 daily advertising messages. By 1997 (the year *Data Smog* was published), that number had swelled to more than 3,000 per day. And at the time of this writing, the Newspaper Association of America proclaimed that the average American was exposed to 3,000 advertising messages *before breakfast*. There's a *lot* of noise out there; to cut through it and convince someone to listen to *you*, you must have a compelling story to tell.

## THE FUNDAMENTALS OF FUNNY

The use of humor can denote an individual's emotions, intelligence, sensitivities, communications skills, and maturity. It's an anodyne for improving relationships and, thus, the potential for persuasion. Plus, when you display a great sense of humor it shows many positive facets of your personality. When you're funny, you have:

1. *Intelligence:* Comedians are bright people. If you disregard the minority of stand-ups who use mindless obscenity in every sentence, you'll find that most comics reveal the core of the human condition and how it relates to politics, sports, health, business, and just about every other aspect of life. Take *The Daily Show*'s Jon Stewart, who builds a fake news broadcast by satirizing the real events of the day. His overwhelming success with that kind of humor didn't happen by accident; Stewart is one of the smartest, most well-read, and provocative comedians working today, which gives him an edge when influencing viewers to agree with his stance on issues ranging from war to equality. In fact, maybe the United States would be better off if *he* ran for national office instead of the politicians he pokes fun at on his show.

2. *Positivity:* Humor generally has an underlying optimism. The subject might be crisis or foolishness, but there's hope at the other end because enough of us still exist to recognize and appreciate the irony. Think about it: The majority of humor derives from pain, mistakes, and unfortunate incidents. Comic expression is the attempt to alleviate that pain, embarrassment, or misfortune. Decades back, Jewish comedians such as Rodney Dangerfield, Joan Rivers, and Milton Berle encouraged their audiences at summer resorts in the Catskill Mountains to laugh at the prejudice they encountered in mainstream society. Great African-American comics like Richard Pryor and Chris Rock helped audiences feel comfortable cackling at the ridiculousness of racism. Female humorists have taken on sexism. Virtually no aspect of society is left untouched. Look to comics to express and expunge the pain of parenting (Jim Gaffigan), job loss (Louis C.K.), obesity (Ricky Gervais), and everyday life (Jerry Seinfeld).

3. *Empathy:* Empathy is the ability to understand and appreciate what someone else is experiencing because you've experienced it yourself (as opposed to "sympathy," which is simply acknowledging another person's hardships and feeling pity or sorrow for them). Humor brings people together to laugh at common foibles and groan over common miseries. Empathic people are among the most likable you'll find. An audience laughing in unison at a humorous story comprises individuals who recognize their close proximity to others in the room.

4. *Perspicacity:* When you can make a witty observation about the complexities of your company's gaining market share in Latin America, it shows you have keen insight and understanding of the nuanced challenges of the situation. Churchill once described Soviet Union foreign policy as "a puzzle inside a riddle wrapped in an enigma . . ." Not a knee-slapper, but certainly good for a chortle. As a matter of fact, I have shamelessly borrowed this line on many occasions to the same result. You should, too.

5. *Creativity:* As mentioned above, humor is an indication of high intelligence, and high intelligence drives creativity. Finding the right degree of irony, satire, self-disclosure, and nuance is not easy, and you don't want humor to become irrational pounding, or irony to become bias.

## STRATEGIC OBJECTIVES OF HUMOR

Humor must be used strategically, and when used wisely it can yield results that will make you smile. Now that you're aware of the fundamentals of humor, here are a few things humor can accomplish:

- *Aid in problem solving:* Humor relieves some of the tension and tendency to assign blame. Instead, it places issues in perspective. People are more likely to consider facts and opinions in the absence of prejudice.

- *Lower your stress level—and that of your persuasion target:* Reducing stress in persuasive situations is invaluable, because stress inhibits talent, accentuates emotionalism over logic, and limits empathy. If both sides are stressed, both will likely be highly defensive, which isn't exactly the royal road to effective communications. (For your consideration: The largest expense for organizations is absenteeism, the largest cause of absenteeism is illness, and the largest cause of illness is stress.)

- *Make you and your ideas more attractive:* Most healthy people like to laugh and are attracted to people who make them laugh. The more effectively you are able to draw people to you in a positive manner, the more open they will be to your ideas. That's the basic math, and that's why stern, dour, and humorless people sometimes repel others; their ideas don't receive a sympathetic ear by default.

## What Humor *Can't* Do

All of that said, humor is not a guaranteed aphrodisiac. There are some cases in which humor will not help you much. For example, humor will not:

- *Overcome polarized opinions:* Bitter enemies will not be mollified by looking at each other's foibles. Likewise, the Hatfields and McCoys were not about to be calmed down with some ironic banter or shrewd displays of sarcasm.

- *Create value where none exists:* If you don't have a sound business case, value proposition, mission statement, beliefs set, or message, humor will not serve as a substitute. Someone running for public office will not be embraced and ultimately elected only because of a clever social media strategy.

- *Enhance credibility:* You're not credible because you're funny; you're funny because you're credible. (Note the chiasmus!) Bob Newhart and Jimmy Kimmel belong on a diverse list of comedians who are funny because we believe in and trust them. Other people who think they're funny but aren't engage in loud and profane behavior, are stuck on one issue, or perform tired gags, and we don't like them. Nothing they can do will change that unless their acts become more credible.

That's why "open mike" nights at comedy clubs can be so punishing. We want Ricky Gervais to be funny to satisfy our belief in him, while strangers who simply claim to be funny virtually never receive the benefit of the doubt. (You're funny? Okay, make me laugh!) The workplace equivalent of "open mike" night is "open mouth" time. The more credibility you have, the more likely your style of humor will be accepted, and the more likely it will help in your persuasion efforts.

Remember, there's a time and a place for humor, and it's not always when and where you think. Sometimes it's just better to keep your mouth shut and let your body do the talking.

## NONVERBAL COMMUNICATION

Physical distance, eye contact, hand and feet positioning, facial expressions, and so forth, all speak more loudly than our mouths. What your body language communicates to your target, and what your target's body language tells you, is the essence of nonverbal power. I call a message that your target sends to you a "nonverbal *tell*" (like in poker when someone has a tendency to, say, look at his watch before he bluffs). Likewise, a "nonverbal *sell*" is a message you send to your target. Recognizing nonverbal tells (NVT) and nonverbal sells (NVS) can be crucial to your persuasion success.

### Nonverbal Tells

Following are the most common tells to watch for—plus how you can interpret them and what you might do in response. A word to the wise:

It is useful to be aware of body language, but don't try to monitor every tic, blink, and grimace. Simply use these tells to get a sense of your target's prevailing winds, not an exact reading on his or her coordinates.

*NVT #1: Solid eye contact.* Your target walks into the meeting room, looking around and smiling, eyes wide and making eye contact with people. This guy knows why he's there, and he's ready for action.

*Response:* Don't miss your opportunity to engage. When you see this sort of tell, mirror the behavior, and ask a question to get a peek into his hand. Two words with an up inflection often will do the trick: "Big day?" "Good week?" "Making progress?" You might be surprised by what you learn.

*NVT #2: Averted eyes.* Now, let's suppose your target is the antithesis of the person above. Maybe he's looking down at his shoes with no distinct facial expression, avoiding eye contact. This guy may think he's entered enemy territory, or is having a bad day. Or perhaps it's just his tendency to be a bit more reserved.

*Response:* Proceed carefully—not boisterously, not aggressively. Don't engage in prolonged eye contact. A brief smile is enough. If you engage, do so with innocuous topics: "Some weather, huh?" (This question works if it's good or bad.) And for heaven's sake, don't force this person to be more outgoing. ("Come on— turn that frown upside down!") Although you can infer some things about a person's disposition from body language, you really have no idea what's going on . . . so give him some space.

*NVT #3: Engaged smile.* Smiling is perhaps one of the only universal signs in body language. Wherever you go on the planet, a warm smile is a positive sign.

*Response:* When your target smiles at you while you're making a point or giving a presentation, reciprocate. Smile, acknowledge her interest, move your gaze to others, and then come back to your smiling target. Holding too long, or focusing too much on her engagement, could make you seem like a weird, desperate stalker who needs a friend as badly as Britney Spears needs another hit. As in most things, moderation is key.

*NVT #4: Dissenting squint.* You know the one. It's often just the slight closing of the eyes, the furrowing of the brow. It's almost a sure sign of disagreement. He may be disagreeing with the point you're making, or disagreeing with something else going on in his head (such as the landscaping advice he got from the guy at the hardware store). The bigger the reaction, the more likely it *is* that he is present and doesn't agree with you.

> *Response:* Here you'll want to bring your target into the conversation. Try a disarming comment followed by a question: "But I might not have all the information. What's *your* take on the situation?"

*NVT #5: Space-saving stance.* If your target, while engaged in conversation with you, seems to be keeping her physical distance or even turning her torso away from you, she either doesn't like your pitch or she's bored.

> *Response:* Tread lightly. This is a clear signal that now is not the right time to talk.

*NVT #6: Watch glance.* When your target looks at his watch, that's about as clear a "tell" as you're going to get. You've asked for the target's time and attention, and now you're not living up to your end of the bargain.

> *Response:* Make your point and get to the ask—*quickly*. If that feels too rushed, buy some time with something like this: "How about I get a bit more information and circle back with you later this week. Does either Thursday or Friday work for you?"

*NVT #7: Restless legs.* Former FBI agent Joe Navarro, in his book *What Every BODY Is Saying* (New York: HarperCollins, 2008), writes that feet and legs are the most likely body parts to reveal a person's true intentions. Targets who shift their feet consistently from the flat to the ready position, bounce their legs, or are literally sitting on the edge of their seats have a ton of energy.

*Response:* Use it! Consider suggesting marching orders, such as: "If you two need to go talk to someone in marketing, now is the time." Or: "If you want to walk over to the R&D building to see the latest iteration of the product prototype, do it." When your target has that much energy, harness it to nudge your request a bit further.

*NVT #8: Eye roll.* If you have a teenage daughter, you're probably very familiar with this impossible-to-misinterpret tell. Difficult to miss, an eye roll definitely means the other person doesn't agree with you or feels as if you're giving her some sort of runaround.

*Response:* Handle this tell immediately, lest you allow the disagreement to fester and become entrenched. Say something like: "I'm sorry, do you not agree?" And you'll find out very quickly what the other person's sticking point is. If she has the chutzpah to roll her eyes in front of you, she will certainly have the gumption to tell you why she disagrees. And that, as Martha Stewart used to say, is a good thing!

### The Eyes Have It

Considering how many scientific studies have been devoted to eyes during the past three decades, perhaps they truly are the windows to our souls. As far back as the 1980s, researchers have claimed that people perceive individuals who engage in eye contact as more trustworthy and likable than those who don't. Research reported by *The New York Times* (www.nytimes.com/2014/05/17/sunday-review/the-eyes-have-it.html?_r=0) and *Psychology Today* (www.psychologytoday.com/blog/cutting-edge-leadership/201404/5-secret-powers-eye-contact) suggests other reasons why, when it comes to persuasion, the eyes have it:

- A genuine smile can be detected by the narrowing of the eyes, creating lines at the outside corners. People who "fake smile" don't have crow's feet.

- Dilated pupils indicate interest. When dilation happens in your target, you'll know you're getting closer to hearing yes.

- Eye contact clears the path to enhanced and more meaningful conversation, because you and your target are now connecting on a stronger level.

Two caveats:

- Some scientists claim that the use of smiley faces and other emoticons in email and text messages is an attempt by the sender to make eye contact with the recipient. Scientists also say this doesn't work.

- Sometimes when engaged in the process of lying, people try too hard to deceive and make *too much* eye contact. "To be liked, you have to make eye contact—but there's a critical amount of eye contact," Peter Hills, a psychologist and eye contact researcher at Anglia Ruskin University in Cambridge, England, told *The New York Times*. "You have to look but not stare."

## Nonverbal Sells

Now that you can recognize and respond to nonverbal *tells*, let's focus on nonverbal *sells*—ways your own body language is sending messages to targets.

*NVS #1: Intentional greetings.* When you shake a target's hand, does your palm face the ground or the ceiling? Your answer to that question says a lot about your persuasion demeanor. Palm facing more downward signals you're in charge of this conversation. Straight up and down, you consider yourself an equal. Palm facing upward, the other person is running the show.

Just make sure that you put something behind that shake. Find a balance between the limp shake and the water-pump or vice-like handshake. And never use the two-handed, now-I'm-going-to-heal-you shake. You know the one I'm talking about. A friendly pat on your target's back also conveys your authority. Just remember: Don't hit hard and repeatedly as if you're trying to help dislodge something from her throat.

*NVS #2: Appropriate distance.* Just like you can infer from your target's distance from you, you communicate your interest with your distance from him. Understand the crucial role distance plays in persuasion. Stand or sit too far away from your target, and you'll seem like a germaphobe. But get too close? Uncomfortable and weird. The best distance for you to make your pitch is at arm's length.

*NVS #3: Thoughtful eye contact.* Make eye contact. Period. Recently, a Harvard University study suggested that eye contact can be intimidating for the other person. That's the dumbest thing I've ever heard. If you can't look me in the eye, I can't trust you. Now, you shouldn't stare your target down like a Bengal tiger hunting for prey, but gazing at your shoes the whole time won't work, either. Find a happy medium: Look at one eye for a while; then break naturally and look at the other eye. This will enable you to maintain powerful eye contact without appearing too intense or creepy.

*NVS #4: Attentive demeanor.* Don't you hate it when you're trying to have a conversation with someone, and that person keeps checking his cell phone? When you are involved in a persuasion conversation, don't even pull your phone out of your pocket—unless you're going to show photos of something pertaining to your pitch. (In fact, if I'm going to a meeting, I've been known to not even take my phone so I won't be tempted.) You can check Facebook and find out what kind of sandwich your friend ate for lunch later.

*NVS #5: Responsive bodily gestures.* Listen with your body. If someone is sharing an intriguing or surprising story with you, show astonishment by widening your eyes, opening your mouth, or tilting your head. If, on the other hand, that person is telling you about a bad experience or something disappointing, grimace, sigh, and shake your head. This conveys empathy, friendliness, and trust much more than a blank stare or slight nod.

*NVS #6: Considered posture.* Research shows that the human brain gives a disproportionate amount of attention to wrists, palms, fingers, and hands. People respond well to hand movements, because if those 10 fingers aren't visible, the thinking is, you have something to hide. So get your hands out of your pockets!

Additionally, Columbia University researchers have linked the way people sit or stand to higher levels of testosterone and lower levels of cortisol, enhancing feelings of power and tolerance for risk. These power poses nonverbally send the message to your target that you are powerful—and create chemical reactions in your body that actually make you feel more powerful. Such "power poses" include standing and leaning on one's hands over a desk as well as sitting with one's legs extended so the feet are on the edge of the desk and hands are behind the head—though you should probably save that one for the privacy of your own office and not, you know, in the office of a senior VP whom you're meeting for the very first time.

*NVS #7: Groomed appearance.* Research shows that you should dress 10 percent better than your target if you want to improve the likelihood of hearing yes. I'm not sure how you would evaluate that sort of sartorial precision, but if you want to perform well, you should dress well. Notice, I said dress 10 percent better—not wear a tux on casual Friday.

One of the most important concepts of nonverbal communication combines your sells and your target's tells; I call it behavioral reflection.

## BEHAVIORAL REFLECTION

I still remember a classic cartoon in *The New Yorker* magazine that depicted a hiring manager and a job candidate sitting across a desk from each other, looking like mirror images. The hiring manager said, "I don't know what it is about you, but I really like you!"

You look like me, and I like that about you. Behavioral reflection can create more agreement, faster. It's imperative to mirror your target's body language, but the key is subtlety. If your target knows he or she is being mimicked, your persuasion prospects are greatly diminished.

It's dangerous to hire, befriend, or support only those people who resemble us, and that's not the point. But making others feel comfortable by your actions is strong persuasion. That can be accomplished by "mimicking" (and I mean that in the best possible sense of the term; mimicking is not "mocking") others' own comfort zones.

The most obvious behavioral reflections include activities you probably already feature in your repertoire: Don't remain seated if someone who is standing begins speaking with you. Smile if the other person smiles in greeting. Show proper facial expressions as the conversation develops. Don't begin eating until everyone at the table has been served and your host begins to eat. Those should be fairly obvious (though in today's educational environment and lax society, you can never be sure). But what about more subtle forms?

Look at the person speaking (there's the eye contact, again) but don't reveal any indication that you might be skeptical or feel exasperated. Don't shift nervously, and do attempt to match the speaker's own level of energy and excitement, or his low-key minimalist nature. This is not manipulative body language; rather it comforts, enhances communication, and strengthens your persuasion power.

Reflect on situations you expect to be in and the people you expect to join you. Rather than constantly interrupt someone who needs to "think out loud," exhibit patience and make that person feel at ease with his own cognitive processes. Similarly, don't demand that someone who doesn't get excited join in your excitement. Moderate your tone and never insist on your own comfort. If people prefer to stand and converse, or chat over a meal, or sit in casual furniture, or walk about the property, join them. The more comfortable they are, the more likely they will be to listen to your case.

In new situations, take time to observe and evaluate the other person's preferences. Mirror what you see. In ongoing situations, prepare accordingly for what you've experienced in the past. The key to the artistry of persuasion is flexibility—not some perfect style or behavioral predisposition. All of this is simple to understand but may require time and practice to perfect. Amazing things can happen when you adjust to environmental conditions in order to make your point.

---

### Chapter 6 Persuasion Points

1. Verbal language involves words, both spoken and written. Master both forms.

2. *What* you say and *how* you say it—steak and sizzle—both matter.

3. Keep your language appropriate for the task, and audience, involved.

4. Use descriptive language.

5. Employ language "tricks," such as metaphors, similes, analogies, and chiasmi, to accelerate acceptance and understanding.

6. Storytelling and humor, when used properly, can be two of the most highly effective persuasion tools.

7. Focus on the "nonverbal sells" and "nonverbal tells" in your interactions.

8. Reflect on how you can generate optimal comfort for those you are trying to persuade.

# Persuasive Processes

## A Five-Step Sequence to Yes

Now it's time for some power calculations. Ready? Remember the Persuasion Equation, which I laid out for you in the Introduction? This is the combination of factors that will add up to your persuasion success. To recap:

(A Great Business Case + Your Outstanding Credibility + Compelling Language) × Intelligent Process = Yes Success

The last three chapters have, in essence, walked you through how to create a great business case, spit shine your credibility, and hone your power language skills. Now it's time to master the persuasive process.

To do this, I'm going to reference another—albeit just slightly more famous—formula: Albert Einstein's Theory of Relativity. Yes, that's right: $E = MC^2$. Well, we know the *formula*, but I'll be smacked if I can find someone who can explain it to me. Luckily, *that's* not on today's agenda. I bring up Einstein only by way of presenting another, similarly structured, formula, one that governs persuasion success: Yes = $E^2F^3$.

In short, Yes = $E^2F^3$ is defined as follows: You get to yes by Engaging your target, Exploring the issue, Forming (and framing) possible options, Finessing any white water, and Finalizing (and formalizing)

the decision. While this formula might seem a little long, it will prove to be a vital component of your overall Persuasion Equation. That's why we're going to spend this chapter walking through each and every step of it together.

## THE PRINCIPLE OF NUDGE

The key to successfully implementing the Yes = $E^2F^3$ formula is what I call the "Principle of Nudge." We're talking about eliciting a series of small agreements—because, after all, persuasion is seldom about evoking one colossal, ear-shattering, cosmic "YES!" People often can be most effectively persuaded when they are shepherded along gently, not yanked through the streets. A great example comes not from a shepherd, but from my sister-in-law's goldendoodle, Lucky.

At one family gathering in their home, Lucky was being particularly affectionate. He kept rubbing against me, looking for attention, which I happily gave him. After a few minutes, I realized I was no longer in the living room, but in the kitchen. When I mentioned my surprise at the change of venue, my sister-in-law replied matter-of-factly: "He does that all the time. He brought you out here; this is where we keep his treats."

*Ah*, the Principle of Nudge.

How might nudge work for you? Let's say your persuasion priority is to convince your VP of marketing to allocate dollars and responsibility to you for a new product training initiative. Here's an example of the series of small agreements you can elicit from your target:

- "Yes, we can meet to talk about your idea."

- "Yes, I can provide information."

- "Yes, I can help brainstorm options."

- "Yes, I can talk to others in my circle to test the idea."

- "Yes, we can run some numbers."

- "Yes, we can pitch the board."

Each yes slowly nudges your target to the big one: "Yes, I'll green-light the project."

In most cases, you wouldn't walk into your VP's office and demand money and power (unless you have an absolutely *monster* credibility and track record, and even then I wouldn't recommend it). That's like asking a person to marry you on the first date. You can, but it doesn't make for good policy.

## THE FIVE-STEP PERSUASION PROCESS

Compare and contrast this:

> *Q:* "Will you have a few minutes next week? I'd like to get your input on something."
>
> *A:* "Sure." (See, you've already got your first yes!)

. . . with this:

> *Q:* "May I have $1.5 million and complete unilateral responsibility for a project you've never heard of?"
>
> *A:* "What is this, an episode of *Punk'd*? Get out of here before I call security!"

The first question suggests an informal, low-pressure exchange of information to which most colleagues would have no problem responding in the affirmative. The second question, however, defies all sense of business decorum and is an immediate turnoff (and surefire way to hear no loud and clear.) The idea behind the five-step persuasion process is to plan for and then guide your target toward the next yes. Like stepping-stones across a stream, this practice can lead you effortlessly from one agreement to the next. The art form here is your judgment. What is the appropriate next step? Well . . .

## Step 1: Engage Your Target

Find the time when your target will be most approachable and receptive. (Remember, here we're talking about one-to-one persuasion attempts; group persuasion will be covered in Chapter 8.) You've heard about how some people shouldn't be bothered until after they've had that first cup of coffee, or how the boss is far less ornery after downing a big lunch. Well, whether it has something to do with personal preferences, biorhythms, or the phases of the moon, some people are more approachable at certain times. (One study showed that Israeli judges were more lenient on sentencing after eating lunch; tough luck for the morning defendants.)

And just as important as *when* is *how* you approach your target. Persuasion relies on relationships, so a face-to-face encounter is always better than a phone call, while an email shouldn't even be considered when it comes to persuasion. Consider those methods three-, two-, and one-dimensional approaches, respectively. Which method of engagement would you most like to encounter when you're being persuaded?

When you're engaging, either go with a formal meeting ("Can we meet at 8:15 in my office?") or what some people call "systematic informality," which is accidentally on purpose bumping into them ("Hey, I'm glad I bumped into you. I have an idea I'd love to discuss.").

The first aspect of engagement involves building (or confirming) rapport. The most ideal situation is when you already know your target well and don't need to do much in terms of establishing a relationship. However, if you *don't* know your target all that well, begin a conversation about a common topic and then eventually transition to the persuasion topic. How do you do that? Mention a project you're working on, offer help, ask for advice, or cite a common experience (maybe you both used to work for a competitor, but at different times). Regardless of your approach, transition to your persuasion topic.

In music, when a song changes to a different key, it's called modulation. Often that shift is subtle (from C to C#, for example) and almost imperceptible to the average listener, but it changes the mood of the piece just slightly. That's exactly what you're doing when you change the energy in the room ever so slightly. You want to build on the rapport you've established and shift the conversation. Here are some tips and language suggestions for a smooth transition:

- *Ask questions:* "What do you think of [the situation you have in mind]?" "Do you have any experience in [the topic}?" You may find out that your target is already closer to your position than you anticipated.

- *Cite a third party* who has asked you about the topic at hand, and inquire as to whether she has been asked.

- *Refer to a publication* in which the persuasion topic was recently mentioned.

- *Ask if your target will be attending a specific meeting* or event related to the persuasion topic.

The engagement aspect is intended to begin a dialogue. I don't advise taking a stance at this point; rather, simply explore the other person's attitudes. Even though you may have been careful in gathering intel during the exercise in Chapter 4, it doesn't hurt to verify your target's viewpoints. One of the persuasion "sins" that people commit is assuming that they absolutely *know* where the other party stands on a certain position. Yet there are Republicans who support Democrats and Democrats who reciprocate. That's because other factors, including geography, constituency, personal experience, and beliefs, can greatly influence perspective.

Another key engagement element is understanding your target's level of knowledge. Has he or she been approached by others regarding the persuasion topic? Read up on it? Had personal experience in dealing with it? Or are you dealing with a blank slate? Keep in mind that independent voters and those on the so-called fence can play a significant role in the outcome of an election, despite the emotion and passion on either side of it.

This is why rapport building is so essential; it increases trust and frees up people to be honest, while also allowing them to reveal additional information. Engaging with another person and not being told the truth is worse than not engaging at all, because then you are likely to act on incorrect or incomplete information. The more time you take to build rapport with your target, the faster you can gain enough engagement to . . .

## Step 2: Explore the Issue

This means delving into its content, as opposed to navigating the approach. The issue is a multifaceted situation, and each facet needs to be considered in turn. First, you need to determine what the issue means to your target, personally and professionally. By personally, I mean issues such as ego, legacy, gratification, self-worth, and off-the-job priorities. By professionally, I'm referring to promotion, remuneration, status, leadership, recognition, and perquisites.

Next, explore what the persuasion topic means to the organization. Is it transformational or minor? Can it mean recovery or market dominance? Will it be widely known and applied, or localized? What are the time implications? Are we talking about a closing window of opportunity? Is there the need to be opportunistic and innovative?

Examine budget parameters. Can this issue be accommodated within the existing budget and, if so, from one source? Or does it require several (and commensurate consensus)? Is the investment unprecedented, or has something similar already been done? Will other issues be delayed or sacrificed because of the investment?

Explore risk, too. Some people have a higher tolerance for risk than others do. Will the desired result, in your target's eyes, justify the identified risk? Can you separate the probability of the risk from its seriousness, so your target can make separate judgments? (Great seriousness can be offset by very low probability, and high probabilities ameliorated by low seriousness.)

With these factors firmly in your mind, explore your target's appetite for the change. Is his interest the same as it has been in the past, or is it enhanced or reduced? Can you suggest preventative actions for any foreseen risks? Have you considered contingent actions for dealing with problems that do arise?

Does your target, having explored the issue with your guidance, offer solutions, new ideas, and insights? Is she clearly excited and willing to take part or even lead? Or does she seem wary and hesitant to commit until others have done so?

All the above questions will garner important early indicators. However, the way in which you ask these questions is critical—you need to engage and explore properly. Remember that persuasion is a science; it's a conversation. Don't interrogate, and don't try to wing it.

Also, don't take sides too early by stating your opinion. Leave room for you to appear as a curious, but well-informed, onlooker. Don't be a zealot seeking to convert; rather, ask follow-up questions for clarity and understanding. Give your target the opportunity to think and respond. And after he or she does respond, count to four and see if your target adds something else. Don't rush to fill the silence. Amazing things can happen in between the conversation.

### Step 3: Form and Frame Possible Options

Onward now to the first of our three "*F*" components: Forming (and framing) possible options. One of my mentors, Alan Weiss, taught me long ago that having options raises the odds of acceptance exponentially. Instead of providing a binary choice—a take-it-or-leave-it option, which is a 50/50 proposition at face value—offering three options raises your chances of acceptance to about 75 percent. In other words, you now have three shots at hearing yes.

**Forming.** Create varied options based on your own exploration information, but also from the responses your target provided during that process. Including some of his comments and observations will substantially increase your odds of success. Try something like this: "Not only should we look for an affiliation in Italy to launch this program, but your idea of sending our own managers over for six-month assignments is a perfect way to develop them and ensure a firsthand view by our own people."

Additionally, most psychologists agree—and my own sales experience concurs—that three is the proper number of options. People tend to think in threes, or "triads," because they are easy to process. Two options are simply binary (this or that), while having more than three options causes decision paralysis. For instance, research shows that television buyers bombarded with dozens of screens on display in a big-box store tend to not buy any of them, because they fear the one they ultimately select might not truly be the right one for them. In scientific experiments, researchers have found that positive impressions peaked at three, and skepticism increased when more points were suggested.

You want to keep options within the target's perceived range of expertise. Hence, three. Years ago, retailers created the "good, better, best" concept. And there's a reason: It works! In fact, you should try that approach to help you form your options.

Let's return briefly to the persuasion priority you articulated on page 11. Think about the various components of the plan and how they might be modified to create a "good," a "better," and a "best" option. What criteria might be modified to form these options? For instance, if you were in a pitch meeting for the Owl Towel project (introduced on pages 71–77), you might vary the initial investment, geographic scope, sales channels, and timing of the rollout—with each successive option being slightly more impressive in each of those four categories than the last. This allows your target to clearly distinguish between the "good" and the "better"—and between the "better" and the "best." Get the idea?

**Framing.** When you present the options you've developed to your target, you need to frame them. Much like certain frames enhance or detract from the attractiveness of a work of art, how you frame your options will impact the likelihood of hearing yes or no. So prepare yourself to be the Renoir of Revenue, and the Picasso of Profit!

Always begin with the most expensive option first. If you do, your target may just select your "best" option. And if she does? Well, that's frost on the beer mug for you and your organization. But the real reason you frame your options in this manner is because your target might say no.

Nobody likes to be turned down, because it feels like failure. But if you have a plan that you can implement in those seconds immediately after rejection, a no can be a lot less painful. This approach is often called "rejection-then-retreat," or as Robert Cialdini sometimes refers to it, "Concessional Reciprocity."

Walking in front of his university library one day, Cialdini was approached by a Boy Scout who asked him if he would like to purchase tickets to the Scouts' circus to be held that Saturday at the local coliseum. The tickets were $5 each. Cialdini politely declined. Without losing an ounce of composure, the boy replied, "Oh, well, then would you like to buy a couple of our chocolate bars? They are only $1 each." Cialdini bought two chocolate bars. Stunned, he knew something significant had just happened—because he doesn't even *like* chocolate!

Analyzing this exchange, Cialdini discovered Concessional Reciprocity—the idea that when you decline someone's offer and that person comes back with a smaller, less extreme offer, you want to say yes to reciprocate for the concession he made to you by accepting your original no.

Wanting to test this idea further, Cialdini took to the streets of Phoenix. Posing as representatives of a youth counseling program, Cialdini and his team approached college students to see if they would be interested in chaperoning a bus trip to the zoo for a group of juvenile delinquents. Seriously! Not surprisingly, 83 percent of them turned him down. (I'd be interested in studying the 17 percent who did respond positively to Cialdini's request!) Cialdini and his research assistants then asked another group of passersby if they would consider something more outlandish. Would they dedicate two hours per week serving as counselors to juvenile delinquents for a minimum of two years? Not surprisingly 100 percent of the prospects turned down this request. When they did, the naysayers were immediately offered the smaller zoo trip request—to which 50 percent agreed, representing a tripling of the prior response rate.

As you can see, it's imperative to have options and frame them accordingly. That way, if your target says no to one, you can retreat to your next offer. Discuss the pros and cons of each option objectively, understanding that they all lead to Rome—that is, your desired outcome. Allow the target to comment critically, perhaps eliminating one option altogether while seriously considering the other two. You might even want to combine aspects of the three options to create one acceptable hybrid. Remember, *all* options are fine with you, because you created them around the goal you're pursuing. Providing choices, any one of which creates the results that you and your target require, is at the heart of forming and framing options, but this doesn't ensure unmitigated success.

## Step 4: Finesse Any White Water

Like rafting through grade five white water, the way in which you navigate resistance to your persuasion attempts will determine your success. Not every target will agree with new ideas (or even old ones). But remember that an objection is a sign of interest; apathy is your real enemy. If your target takes the time to express counterarguments, skepticism, or doubt, she is engaged enough to invest her time.

Thus, objections are a good sign. Below are the categories of typical objections and what you can do to rebut them. These are phrased in the classic "no" method, meaning your target says, "We have 'no need' for such a plan." And that's where we'll begin:

**No need.** Just because *you* see a need, doesn't mean others will. Needs are hardly universal, so you must create need in the eyes of your target. Use the categories we've noted previously (personal, professional, organizational, and so forth). Highly persuasive people possess strong capabilities of creating need among others. Find and demonstrate alternate uses that your target hasn't yet considered. (For instance, the training program won't just develop people in our retail channel, but can be used to develop our internal field sales force and customer service people as well.)

**No money.** This is probably the oldest and most common objection. "We just don't have the money." How many times have you heard that? Money, however, is not a resource; it's a priority. That means there is *always* money. The real question is, to whom is it provided? After all, the lights are on, payroll is being met, the plants are being misted, and the parking lot is routinely getting cleaned. The point of persuasion is to ensure that existing money is provided for your persuasion priority, as opposed to something else. Consequently, making your position a *high priority* is essential.

Some alternatives for you are to justify the investment (see how important that ROI section in Chapter 4 is now?), explain alternate forms of payment (different departments could share in the expense, or it could be broken down over different financial quarters), or even break down the costs so they are more palatable. Few people buy a $50,000 vehicle; they buy a vehicle for $500 a month.

**No time.** Sometimes referred to as "no hurry" (as in, "We're in no hurry to say yes to your idea."). This argument—"We just don't have the time"—is as specious as no money. There is always time. Every day contains 24 hours. The question is, what priorities will that time be relegated to? If someone says there is no time, what he means is there is no urgency, which implies that other issues have higher priorities. Hence, it's up to you to elevate the urgency. You have to prove to your target why saying yes now benefits him. Is there a window of opportunity in the marketplace? Is there a particular resource in the organization that is available now but won't be later? Is the mood of the organization ripe for this sort of initiative?

**No trust.** This is the really big one. No matter how much need, money, and time I have, I'm not going to support you or your position if I don't trust you. Trust is a function of your target believing that you understand her position (empathy) and will help her achieve her self-interests rather than manipulate them.

As we mentioned earlier, signs of trust include sharing humor, requesting opinions, revealing details not asked for, accepting pushback, and offering assistance. Trust can be gained in 20 minutes, after three meetings, or, sometimes, never. So here you have to keep your promises, not rush, prove your capabilities, and use third-party endorsements (and the Halo Effect!) to establish your credibility.

A final consideration is personality styles. (Remember the discussion about Drivers, Expressives, Amiables, and Analyticals that we introduced on pages 48–50? We're coming back to those four categories now.) You need to tailor your argument to suit the particular objection for the personality profile of your target. See the personality/objection matrix in Figure 7-1.

### The ART of Persuasion

To be successful with the five-step persuasion process you must package each step using your language skills to finesse your way through some challenging conversations. That's when my ART of Persuasion model comes in handy. When facing one of the objections mentioned above, you'll want to:

- *Acknowledge the objection.* Doing so psychologically prepares your target to hear your message.

- *Respond in a substantive and compelling manner,* using three key pieces of information and interesting figures of speech.

- *Transition to your next nudge.* Where else do you want to take the conversation?

(Continued on next page)

*(Continued from previous page)*

Here's an example: "Your new product training idea is too expensive."

*"I understand completely. At first I thought it seemed expensive, too, but then I discovered key information that changed my mind, and it might change yours. There are three reasons the program makes sense.*

*"First, with this program, we will improve the skills of our entire retail channel. It's like getting three or four development programs for the price of one.*

*"Second, I've crunched some numbers, and we should have finance check them out. But if through this effort we can increase retail sales by just 1 percent globally as a result of better training, that would add an additional $15 million to product revenues. That would give this program a 10:1 return!*

*"Finally, we don't want to waste all the effort required getting this product to market just to lose it with an uninformed retailer. We don't want to quit the marathon right in front of the finish line. If we don't take care of the market launch, the market may just launch our product.*

*"What do you think?"*

There's a lot going on in this example, so let me break it down. Here we demonstrated the ART of Persuasion (Acknowledge, Respond, Transition), and we used our rebuttal strategies from above (justifying costs). We also went back to the case-building chapter and referenced ROI ratios; we leveraged Cialdini's principle of scarcity (not wanting to waste effort); and we even delved into our power language toolbox to incorporate metaphor (the marathon) and a chiasmus ("If we don't take care of the market launch, the market may just launch our product.")

Ending the above example with "What do you think?"—well, that takes us to the fifth and final step. . .

**Figure 7-1** Personality/Objection Matrix

| | Driver | Expressive | Amiable | Analytical |
|---|---|---|---|---|
| **No Need** | Raise the performance bar (e.g., Raised sales 10 percent? Who says it shouldn't have been 12 percent?) | Show how other people she knows have used in a unique way. | Show how others in the same peer group have used to their advantage. | Let him do the math behind the performance improvement; he'll believe it if he does it. |
| **No Money** | Prove how she can quickly source the funds or pay down the obligation. | Show how not going ahead will cause him to lose status or market position. | Prove how this will protect her investment (e.g., the resale value or yearly return). | Help him break down into monthly or yearly figures; avoid daily breakdowns, as Analyticals resist those. |
| **No Time** | Indicate how acting now will enable her to accomplish her goal faster. | Show why going ahead will keep him with his social group. | Point out how acting now will keep her at "par" with her peers. | Don't rush unnecessarily (he needs time to (process), but at the same time, point out what's lost if decision takes too long. |
| **No Trust** | Show how other people in similar businesses have used to their advantage. | Show how others she respects have done what you're suggesting. | Demonstrate how you have interacted with a known and trusted peer. | Use a well-known, objective, and respected third-party media source. |

## Step 5: Finalize and Formalize the Decision

Ask for your target's opinion—not for a commitment. Opinions are nonthreatening: Everyone has them, and most want to share them. Simply say, *"What do you think?"*

If you receive a positive response ("I really like the "best" option you've created"), move boldly forward. Finalize and formalize the decision: "Perfect! I'll have the purchase order on your desk by the end of the day." And consider yours a persuasion success story.

If you receive a neutral response ("I'm still not sure"), don't try right away to secure your yes. You have more work to do. Instead, say something along the lines of: "I understand completely. Here's what I'm going to recommend. Don't say yes. Don't say no. Let's just make sure we're clear about what we're talking about and willing to consider it further. Fair enough?"

What reasonable person wouldn't say yes to *that*? Most will. And guess what? That's called a "nudge."

Ask your target why he or she isn't sure and what would lead to greater confidence. Is information missing? Would your target like to see additional people backing your persuasion position? Does a formal plan need to be presented?

If you receive a flat-out no, employ your options: "Okay, if you don't want to go with the training program for the entire North America distribution channel, perhaps we should just do Retailers and Field Sales Force. Or, if you prefer, just the Field Sales Force. Which of these options would you suggest?"

When formed, framed, and finessed, I like our chances of hearing yes. They're getting better with every move. Nonetheless, there are still other considerations to keep in mind: Somewhere among a no, a neutral, and a yes response lurk mysterious X factors—such as technological glitches, competitive actions, and intrusions by a trusted adviser—that seemingly come from out of nowhere to derail your persuasion efforts. You'll want to uncover any X factors before leaving this phase of persuasion.

Never accept a simple yes. Instead work toward a profound agreement. I call this the *"Columbo* method." Actor Peter Falk played a disheveled TV detective named Lt. Columbo who became known for extracting the info he needed from sources by saying, "One more thing before I go . . ."

So take a cue from Columbo: "Is there anything we haven't discussed that will prevent us from moving forward?" "Will you be having conversations with others who might not have the insight from our exchanges?" "In the past, has anything surfaced at the last minute to change your mind about decisions like this?"

And then you want to formalize the decision. By that, I mean you want your target to somehow go on record with his decision. Of course, for many this means a signed contract. For others it may mean issuing a purchase order. At the very least you want your target to send an email or, in conversations, tell others. This formalizes your agreement and can make it stick. Once a person goes on record, he or she will do just about anything to stick with that commitment.

## WORKING FAST OR SLOW

How long will this take? These five components of this persuasion process (engage, explore, form/frame, finesse, and finalize/formalize) can be accomplished in one conversation or over a matter of days, weeks, or even months. Everything from personality to position on the issue can impact how long an effort might be required. As we mentioned previously, rarely do people change their minds in a Paul-on-the-road-to-Damascus manner. But keep in mind that once you frame your target's options, you'll want to close in fast.

Consider these steps a guide. After all, everyone needs a guide: Sir Edmund Hillary had Sherpa Tenzing Norgay to help him reach the summit of Mount Everest. Explorers Meriwether Lewis and William Clark had Sacagawea as an interpreter and guide as they navigated their way into the untamed lands of the western United States. Let this model be your guide as you move toward accomplishing your persuasion priority. It's specific enough to provide key direction, yet flexible enough for your own interpretation. Leveraging a well-strategized process will accelerate your path to yes.

---

### Chapter 7 Persuasion Points

1. Remember the formula Yes = $E^2F^3$. You get to yes by engaging your target, exploring the issue, forming and framing possible options, finessing any white water, and finalizing and formalizing the decision.

2. Engagement is the act of becoming approachable and determining when others are approachable.

3. Exploration is the investigation of what is important to your target.

4. Forming and framing options enable the "choice of yeses," which vastly increases your persuasion ability.

5. Finessing the white water includes overcoming the four objections most commonly encountered: need, money, time, and, most important, trust.

6. Time and money are priorities, not resources.

7. Depending on the circumstances, the persuasion process can be accelerated. But it also may need to obey a caution flag every now and then.

8. Consider this chapter your navigation guide to leveraging your speed and ensuring your direction.

# Persuasion 360

## How to Get Agreement Up, Down, and All Around

Thus far, we've focused on persuading just one target. Now we're going to turn our attention to persuading groups and specific members of groups. The first thing you need to acknowledge is that group decisions don't get made in group settings. Think about that. It's counterintuitive but inescapably true. Groups hear and discuss, sometimes debate and argue, but they seldom decide as a unit. Rarely will you find a single decision maker. Rather, multiple decision makers—often including, but not limited to, the budget manager, a hierarchical leader, and an informal leader—are involved in the final decision.

Thus, you need to appeal to fiscal prudence, leadership responsibility, charisma, or all of the above. Group meetings must be augmented by one-on-one meetings to gain support and woo true decision makers. Consider yourself a congressional lobbyist, but one with scruples and a good cause.

You don't need unanimity or an overwhelming mandate to generate group agreement; you need critical mass. Consensus is something everyone can live with, not something everyone would die for. With that in mind, focus on the pragmatism of the numbers. That means "being right" in your own mind isn't sufficient. You may have all the facts, all the right conclusions, but that still doesn't mean your idea will become reality in a group setting. You must be cajoling and politically savvy; you must "work" the system, just as you would "work" a room when you're networking. You don't want to meet everyone, just the people who can help you the most. (A politician wants to convince every voter to vote for him or her but is most interested in those voters who can deliver—through their own influence—thousands of additional votes. Hence, a union officer is more attractive to a politician than a union member.) This is the kind of persuasive thinking that must go on in your head *all the time*.

## WHERE PEOPLE STAND DEPENDS
## ON WHERE THEY SIT

Group targets who are idealists will try to tell you how the organization should work, while those who are pragmatists will tell you how things actually do work and how best to leverage that reality. American presidents Bill Clinton and Ronald Reagan were pragmatists in office, while presidents Jimmy Carter and Barack Obama were idealists. The differences in legislation passed and congressional support during their terms are overwhelming.

Groups are not sentient creatures as an entity but comprise sentient creatures. The legal and marketing departments will have different views on your pitch than, say, the R&D and finance departments will. (Inevitably, the human resources staff will always present alternate views and be the so-called odd man out.) Where others stand on an issue depends on the professional background they bring to the discussion and the impact that yes will have on their jobs, ranks, or careers.

One of the weaknesses of group influence is that the task takes much longer because of such dynamics. You have to stay the course and, in some cases, outlast opponents who will eventually be transferred, promoted, retired, terminated, or otherwise obscured or overruled. Sometimes no other way exists, so be prepared for a long-term persuasion arrangement, if necessary, in which you'll need to create allies who recognize how they can prosper from your ideas.

## SELF-TEST: WHAT IS YOUR PERSUASION IQ?

*Horsepower. Pull. Sway.* These words should be used to describe your organizational Persuasion Influence Quotient (or "Persuasion IQ"). (As covered earlier, I consider "persuasion" to be an action and "influence" to be a state or a condition.) Influence reflects the ability to create an effect without exerting an effort. The ability to persuade up, down, or all around depends significantly on your influence—and, frankly, has precious little to do with your title or ranking in the organization. How do *you* measure up?

### Evaluating Your Skill Sets

Following are 11 ways in which you can evaluate your Persuasion IQ. Don't overthink your answers, and don't search for surgical precision. Just answer the questions, completely and honestly.

1. Do others in your organization regularly ask for your opinion?

   Never                    Sometimes                    Often
   1     2     3     4     5     6     7     8     9     10

2. Have you been asked repeatedly to present your ideas, projects, or results to your organization's senior management? (And, no, if you are a senior manager, talking to yourself does not count.)

   Never                    Sometimes                    Often
   1     2     3     4     5     6     7     8     9     10

3. Have you been cited in outside media for your positive contributions?

   Never                    Sometimes                    Often
   1     2     3     4     5     6     7     8     9     10

4. Have you been asked to speak to industry trade groups?

Never                    Sometimes                    Often
1      2      3      4      5      6      7      8      9      10

5. Are you invited to weigh in on future company initiatives?

Never                    Sometimes                    Often
1      2      3      4      5      6      7      8      9      10

6. Have others asked you to informally mentor them?

Never                    Sometimes                    Often
1      2      3      4      5      6      7      8      9      10

7. Do your peers repeatedly use you as a sounding board?

Never                    Sometimes                    Often
1      2      3      4      5      6      7      8      9      10

8. Have you been formally asked to play a role in your organization's leadership development?

Never                    Sometimes                    Often
1      2      3      4      5      6      7      8      9      10

9. Are you actively involved in the design and execution of company or work group policy?

Never                    Sometimes                    Often
1      2      3      4      5      6      7      8      9      10

10. Are you invited by powerful people in your organization to get together socially?

Never                    Sometimes                    Often
1      2      3      4      5      6      7      8      9      10

11.  Do you believe that people speak about you in an overwhelm-
     ingly positive way when you're not present?

     Never                    Sometimes                    Often
     1     2     3     4     5     6     7     8     9     10

### Interpreting Your Results

Add up your score, and divide by 11. This is your Persuasion IQ score.

1–3: Your Persuasion IQ is Low.

3–6: Your Persuasion IQ is Medium.

6–8: Your Persuasion IQ is High.

9+: Your Persuasion IQ is Superior.

Does the title on your business card have something to do with your
organizational pull? Of course it does. But it's not the most powerful
factor. People who rely on their position for their power base typically
don't enjoy great careers, which is why no matter where you are in your
organization (or even if you are an entrepreneur), this test can help determine the way to get more sway.

## SEVEN WAYS TO "INFLUENCE UP"

Your ability to influence multiple targets will take many forms, requiring you to "influence up" (your boss, shareholders, a client's president)
and "influence down" (an outside organization, a temporary aide, a con-
tracted employee). First, I present to you seven ways to influence up
(which, incidentally, work well in individual persuasion situations, too):

1. *Speak the language.* How do your targets view their work and
   their environment? Do they talk about market share, Return
   on Investment, Return on Equity (ROE), risk mitigation, competitive advantage, Market Intelligence (MI), shareholder value,

stakeholder opinion, media response, or global presence? Make sure to cast your arguments in your targets' language; interpret your goals for acquiring increased development funds in terms of higher market share and make a case for achieving a strong ROI in a brief time span.

2. *Deal with evidence, not opinions.* Assemble the facts and remember that we're talking about rules, not exceptions. Frequency of occurrence helps support facts and separate anomalies. Make sure your points are evidence-based and as unassailable as the rule.

3. *Find workable approaches.* As stressed previously, don't threaten people with an inquisition. Seek ways to rectify and reconcile so that everyone finds the solution salutary and satisfying. "Witch hunts" do not encourage people to emerge in the daylight with facts and suggestions.

4. *Be concise.* Don't tell people everything you know; tell them only what they need to know. (Otherwise, this book would be 5,000 pages long—to my editor's considerable chagrin!) You need your targets' attention, not their captivity. So ensure that you can succinctly state your case in the allocated time. Some people actually articulate their cognitive processes by "thinking out loud." This horrible practice wastes time and diverts attention. Which brings us to . . .

5. *Manage the clock.* If you end a meeting 10 minutes early, nobody is going to complain. But if you run over the allocated time by 2 minutes, people will rapidly lose interest—even if you held their undivided attention 3 minutes ago. To avoid that, work backward, allowing the final 10 minutes of a designated time frame to be used to develop consensus, determine next steps, set times and dates, and assign accountabilities. These are busy folks, with other places to be and people to see.

6. *Stand your ground.* Maintain the courage of your position, meaning that while you should remain open to other views and even criticism, don't back down in the face of strong opposition or peer pressure. People are most prone to follow formal and informal leaders who can both take the heat and lead the way through ambiguity and resistance.

7. *Relish being the contrarian.* "Yes men" are abundant in organizations—don't forget, we're talking about group persuasion here—and they always attempt to side with the status quo to remain in the boss's good graces. If you want to truly succeed at persuasion, be willing to stand out and be identified as someone with ideas that don't adhere to the overused slogan, "That's how we've always done things."

These best practices to "influence up" are based on boldness and brevity, which strong senior people tend to appreciate and respond to positively. Remember that the people with whom you are dealing in group persuasion environments are paid to achieve results, and the quickest, most obvious road to that success will strike harmonious chords. So make your case in their language with an outcome-based focus in as brief a time as possible.

### When Consensus Is Overrated

Sometimes the most compelling path to persuasion isn't via group buy-in. In fact, dissension in the ranks can establish you as a bolder leader.

Leaders are paid to achieve results. Period. They often, therefore, must make tough decisions—decisions that others might shy away from or try to drown in a group setting. U.S. Army General Dwight D. Eisenhower didn't call a meeting before launching the D-

*(Continued on next page)*

*(Continued from previous page)*

Day invasion of Europe, and US Airways pilot Chesley "Sully" Sullenberger III didn't ask permission from the control tower prior to landing Flight 1549 in the Hudson River after geese disabled the engine power.

In other words, leadership doesn't happen by committee. When the situation warrants, you need to make the tough call. So the next time you're in a meeting and consensus over your ask seems unforthcoming, be the voice of reason for the group and render a decision that you know will result in the right outcome. You lead by creating results from which the majority will benefit—even if the majority doesn't agree with you at that moment.

## SEVEN WAYS TO "INFLUENCE DOWN"

Now let's look at the opposite of influencing up, which is "influencing down" the hierarchical ladder. You don't want people merely following orders or feeling coerced, because you're likely to attain compliance but not commitment. Instead, you want enthusiastic supporters who demonstrate innovation and passion for their work and the outcomes. Here are seven ways to influence down (which, like those for influencing up, also work well in individual persuasion situations):

1. *Use your "home field advantage."* As mentioned previously, your office is the perfect place to persuade, especially if you and your targets are surrounded by your honors, awards, and diplomas—which subtly show the power of your position. Showcase your authority and remain more comfortable than anyone else in your own surroundings. (Obviously, if you work in a cubicle or you're pitching to a large group, you'll need to find an alternate location. In that case, a neutral space, such as a conference room or an off-site location, might work best.)

2. *Avoid condescension at all costs.* Treat everyone as a rational adult by never implying a concept or topic is above someone else's

"pay grade." Keep your voice confident, low-pitched, and professional, and avoid "up talk" at the end of sentences (ending the sentence on a higher pitch than you began, making declarative statements sound like interrogatives).

3. *Be brief but not abrupt.* Take time to entertain questions. Pay as much attention and invest as much time with this process as you would if you were influencing up. Don't expend less energy on these folks simply because they have lesser positions.

4. *Leverage honest ingratiation.* In other words, sweet-talk your targets: "Your team has an exceptional track record with this marketing campaign, and I'd like your support in taking the initiative to the next level, because I know you guys can handle the added responsibilities." If you're honest and sincere, this is a fine tactic. If you're neither, then it's merely manipulative and will be unethical, ineffective, and perhaps even counterproductive.

5. *Request input.* Don't just ask for positive feedback, but invite negative comments, too, about what weaknesses your targets can detect in your pitch: "What do you see as the main vulnerabilities of this marketing plan?" It's far more effective to elicit views regarding both sides of the issue rather than blindly believing your idea is perfect (or at least the only option).

6. *Provide opportunities for contributions.* The majority of people would prefer to have control and influence over their work than regular pay raises, so explore how latitude of action and independence could help sway opinion: "We need someone to organize the database, work with the agency on calendar issues, and write the sales force communication. Which of these tasks would you most prefer?" In fact, application of talents and recognition for accomplishments are two of the primary motivators in the workplace. Why? Because people love autonomy. Incorporate that need into your plans whenever possible as another way of appealing to others' self-interests.

7. *Don't micromanage.* I call this approach allowing "freedom with fences." You delegate to subordinates all the time with the intent of reducing your own labor intensity, and the same dynamic applies here. Set aside some time to provide feedback, of course, as well as monitor and fine-tune results, while still remembering that autonomy often drives employees. (Feedback isn't necessarily something all employees want, but it's something you should know they *need*.)

## FIVE WAYS TO "INFLUENCE SIDEWAYS"

Well, now that we've addressed your supervisors and subordinates, one last group of targets remains: your peers. This is known as "influencing sideways." Peer pressure is among the strongest of all propulsions in the workplace (and elsewhere). How can you leverage it? Here are five ideas:

1. *Cultivate favors by doing favors.* Remember the scene in *The Godfather* where Don Corleone agrees to help the undertaker handle an issue with his daughter, and then calls upon him much later for a return favor with a dead body? You can make people an "offer they can't refuse," because they are obligated to you. But this requires you to do well by others first—creating, say it with me, re•ci•pro•city. A *quid pro quo*. Whose *quid* and whose *quo* can be worked out later. People respond to obligations.

2. *Link agendas.* By this, I mean that you should strive to forge common goals in an attempt to initiate persuasion. Employees at a tech start-up, for example, might think they serve two very different customers: the hardware providers and the end users. But there clearly exist areas of overlap, such as eye-popping graphics and the goal of seamless integration. Find the common areas of fulfillment with peers to then share ideas and resources. These may involve people, money, information, or facilities.

The cost to you is minimal; the effect, potentially substantial.

3. *Leverage loss aversion.* This may sound harsh, but leveraging the aversion to loss is a key factor in navigating peer pressure. Helping peers feel protected from loss of status, talent, income, and market opportunities can significantly impact on your desired outcome. Allow people to see that your intentions are comforting, not threatening, and they'll remember.

4. *Covet your credibility.* The fastest path to yes within all of this is your credibility. The more your peers can rely on your past behavior, track record, honesty, and commitment, the more likely they will be to accept your claims, offers, and pitches. Trust wins the day when your peers have experienced positive outcomes with you in the past.

5. *Be fair.* Ensure that, in reality and in perception, the support you seek is not unilateral. Make it clear and obvious that no one (most important, you!) is taking advantage of anyone else. Insist on establishing a win-win dynamic.

## DEALING WITH DECEIT

Give others the benefit of the doubt until proven otherwise. This will allow you to be sure your suspicions are not motivated by envy or otherwise. Don't be paranoid, either. People who don't jump on your bandwagon early aren't necessarily opposed to your pitch; they just may not appreciate the wagon yet.

Occasionally, some people do think only of themselves and attempt to thwart your persuasion efforts for self-aggrandizing reasons. They take credit for what's not theirs, manipulate others, and seem concerned only with personal advancement. They could act in a passive-aggressive manner by seemingly taking your side but then constantly undermining you through faint praise and nuanced critiques.

When that happens, control your emotion. Deceitful people can offend your sense of judgment to such a degree that you're motivated to go head-to-head with them on an issue in a public setting. Don't. That's what they want you to do (because most of them are pragmatists, not idealists). A public—or at least an office—feud, whether you win or lose, will delay and often derail your persuasion plans. Most feuds simply meander on interminably, with no resolution and with others rapidly losing interest or at least feeling uncomfortable in group settings. Additionally, your opponent is likely skilled in the art of deception and will turn public conversations around as if to question your intentions.

One effective strategy against feuding is containment. Keep other options in your pocket to accomplish tasks without opponents' input. Isolating their opposition or foot-dragging to minor issues, while gaining momentum on the major elements of your persuasion effort, will allow you to make necessary headway—much like the army that maneuvers around a single island of resistance on the way to its ultimate goal.

Another option is to shine a spotlight on the deceitful. In meetings with others, ask the deceiver to discuss his concerns. While it's easy to be deceitful, it is much more difficult to present facts and figures to defend the deception. This is why group meetings play an important role in honest persuasion exploration. A final option is to not wait for the deceitful person to place his agenda items at the end of the meeting, because he knows that's when the rubber stamp comes out and people are eager to move on. If you are able to move those items higher up on the agenda, you will control the conversation.

And once you control the conversation, you're that much closer to obtaining agreement from groups.


## NAVIGATING THE POLITICAL TERRAIN

If you want to dramatically improve your ability to persuade groups of people, you must learn how to wrap your head around two key words: *organizational politics*. If there are two words that evoke stronger disdain from professionals in organizational life today, I've not encountered them. But one man I met early in my career enabled me to rethink organizational politics. The late Joel DeLuca received his Ph.D. from Yale University in organizational behavior, led organizational development initiatives at companies that eventually became known as Sunoco and PricewaterhouseCoopers, and taught leadership at the Wharton School of the University of Pennsylvania. In 1992, he wrote *Political Savvy: Systematic Approaches to Leadership Behind-the-Scenes* (Horsham, PA: LRP Publications), and in 2000 he taught me how to map the political terrain of an organization so I could achieve my persuasion aims.

Now I'm going to teach you. (Hint: It helps to have a map.)

### Mastering Political Territory Mapping Techniques

One of the challenges when trying to bring a group of people on board with an initiative is the seemingly overwhelming amount of information exchanged. Who said what to whom at what meeting? How entrenched are his or her positions? Who knows whom, and who thinks what of whom? Let's face it. Most organizations would make a great setting for a television soap opera. But you don't have the time, energy, or resources to sit back and watch the ever-evolving Days of Our Office Lives play out. You need a picture of the political landscape in front of you. Welcome to Joel DeLuca's Political Territory Mapping technique (or what I refer to as "Persuasion GPS!").

Looking at the top of the map (Figure 8-1), you'll see "Applied Influence," which is subdivided into two sides: "Against" and "For." Across the top are degrees of "against-ness" and "for-ness." When filling this out you won't need surgical precision; your best guess will suffice. Have your targets demonstrated stridently and publicly that they are against your idea? If so, you might rate them as –8, –9, or even a –10. If, on the other hand, some of your targets have been leaning toward supporting your idea all along but need a bit more information before they're completely convinced, place them on the "for" side somewhere between +3 and +5.

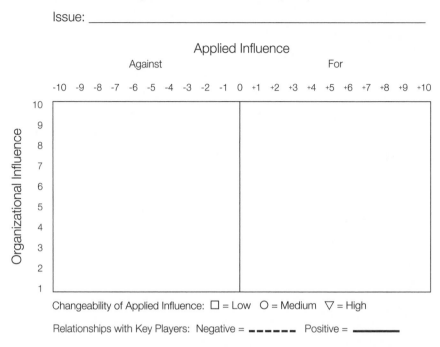

**Figure 8-1** Political Territory Map

The axis identified on the left side of the map asks you to evaluate your targets' "Organizational Influence," or organizational horsepower. Again, no need for pinpoint accuracy; just a decent approximation will get you there. Next, outline what DeLuca called "Changeability": What is the likelihood that your targets will change their minds—low, medium, or high? You will indicate that by simply outlining each player's name in the appropriate shape. Finally, evaluate any unusually positive relationships with a solid line and any unusually negative relationships with a dashed line. Voilà! Now you have an effective snapshot of what you're facing.

## TRANSFORMING THEORY INTO PRACTICE

Now, let's see how this map works by reviewing the office politics at a fictional software company called Retail Solutions, Inc. Let's say the president has appointed a new marketing director, named Sheila. He didn't run his plan by David, the marketing VP, prior to the appointment; he just placed Sheila in the position (sometimes colloquially called a "slam dunk").

She's now eager to prove to the organization that she's competent and deserving of the position, and she has some radical new ideas in terms of software products. Because the president pulled executive privilege to secure the appointment, Sheila's not without ample horsepower. But not many employees in the organization know or trust her (though an attorney named Allison works well with her).

A major retailer already wants the new software Sheila has proposed, but appeasing that client would require crashing project timelines. Sheila pushes hard for the organization to put everything on hold to support her project and this huge opportunity—requiring enormous sacrifice and risk for the organization.

Few in the organization are in favor. Matt, the director of software design (and the organization's 800-pound gorilla), distrusts Sheila, because one of his greatest software projects was destroyed as a result of "crashing." To say he is against Sheila's proposal to crash the project is like saying Boston Red Sox fans have a slight disregard for the New York Yankees.

David thinks the hurry-up required will unfairly take budget dollars from other, more deserving projects, but he's reasonable in his position. David has been employed by Retail Solutions for a long time and has close ties to the CFO, Eric, who also is leaning against the project. Either way, both of these guys pull considerable sway in the organization. The only person not publicly against the project is Eric's trusted colleague Allison (the attorney), but she's so consumed with improving the reputation of the legal department that she's staying out of this debate.

Yikes! Now *that's* a mess. At least it is until you apply the Political Territory Mapping approach. Then it looks like the map in Figure 8-2.

Although not a Persuasion Action Plan yet, the map does cut through the organizational noise and enable you to view the landscape within which you are operating. From here, if you follow the positive relationships and speak to others' enlightened self-interest, you have the beginning of a Persuasion Action Plan.

**Figure 8-2** Retail Solutions, Inc.

Issue: _____

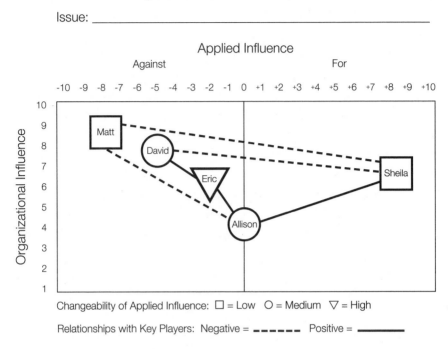

Changeability of Applied Influence: ☐ = Low   ○ = Medium   ▽ = High

Relationships with Key Players:  Negative = ▬ ▬ ▬ ▬ ▬    Positive = ▬▬▬▬▬

To finish our story, Sheila put the map to good use. She leveraged her tight relationship with Allison to sway Eric and David to see things her way—and that, in turn, snowballed into such power momentum that she got the green light on her project.

The map is a terrific tool and can substantially reduce the time and energy it takes for you to separate the organizational wheat from the chaff. It focuses attention, identifies critical relationships, and enables you to test your assumptions with other politically savvy–minded people.

Are there caveats? Sure. The map is static. It's just a snapshot of your ever-moving organization. Also, sometimes numbers give the impression of accuracy. Joel DeLuca used to joke about engineers going to three decimals in terms of evaluating someone's organizational horsepower. ("She's a 7.765!") But just because you've done that doesn't mean your evaluation is any more or less accurate. It's still an approximation based on your own judgment.

Be careful not to overuse the map; this technique should be employed only occasionally and for big issues—not for deciding where to go for lunch. There also is the issue of confidentiality. You may use Political Territory Mapping with a small cadre of people who are close to you, but you wouldn't post the map in the cafeteria. Regardless, the strengths greatly outweigh any weaknesses. Mapping allows you to develop persuasive strategies in half the time, think beyond the obvious, and bypass some of the organizational white water.

The map isn't a hammer you'll use every day, but it should definitely be in your toolbox. Having the ability to get agreement up, down, and all around is the ultimate skill for any persuasion professional. Practice the techniques presented here and you will be a persuasion professional par excellence.

---

### Chapter 8 Persuasion Points

1. Remember that group decisions don't get made in group settings.

2. You must influence up, down, and sideways.

3. Focus on solutions and admirable goals.

4. Consensus does not mean unanimity.

5. Treat everyone equally—as rational adults.

6. Some people can be convinced, while others can help convince several people.

7. Use reciprocity and obligation when persuading groups of targets.

8. Prepare for the occasional deceitful opposition by asking for supporting evidence and controlling the conversation.

9. Learn and use Political Territory Mapping so you can clearly see the direction you need to travel to get group agreement.

# Persuasion 911

## What to Do When Your Persuasion Attempts Go Awry

I've flown considerably more than a million airline miles, and I've never taken a single flight that didn't have at least *some* turbulence during the ascent. Likewise, rarely do persuasion attempts get off the ground without at least a few bumps. I call this "assent turbulence."

Persuasion turbulence occurs when new information appears, people are influenced by other opinions, or X factors are in play. Be it a promotion, a firing, or a merger, things happen that change a person's perspective on your request. And the larger (or more complex) your request is, the more important it is for you to buckle your seat belt. But just because things get a bit bumpy doesn't mean your flight won't ultimately arrive at your intended destination. You simply need strategies for navigating "assent turbulence." This chapter explores the inevitable bumps on your ascent to assent.

## TROUBLESHOOTING THE SEVEN MOST COMMON WEAKNESSES IN A PITCH

If you've agreed with (and put into action) even half of what we've covered in this book so far, you will dramatically decrease the assent turbulence you experience as your persuasive efforts take flight. That said, I'm not going to guarantee a completely smooth transition to yes. Here are seven factors that contribute to persuasion taking a wrong turn:

1. *Lack of trust:* You'll know that trust is missing if your target fails to be forthcoming with information, asks for delays, acts guarded, and is curt and abrupt in responses—or worse, doesn't ask any follow-up questions.

   *Response:* Be 100 percent candid with your target, and address the elephant in the room: "Mike, we don't seem to be on the same page with this issue, but it is important to both of us. So let's be honest, see if we can forge a compromise, and be allies rather than adversaries." Or this: "Monica, you seem hesitant. Why don't we talk frankly about your concerns so we can both be more comfortable?" Ask people for the "favor" of honesty, trust, and patience, and, as Ben Franklin advised, they'll return the favor and trust you more in the process.

2. *Lack of value:* This is indicated by no clear economic Return on Investment, no personal benefit for the target, and no attempt to link qualitative returns to actual evidence. Value, as they say, is in the eye of the beholder. And the other person's eye is the one that needs to behold the benefits of your pitch.

   *Response:* Have your target stipulate what an effective return would be, at least theoretically. What would he like to see happen? Start with the ROI and work backward, being sure to turn qualitative benefits into quantitative metrics whenever possible. (For more on this, revisit Chapter 4.)

3. *Lack of clarity:* You'll know your pitch isn't working when you're hit with a slew of questions, insistence on qualifiers, digressions, and a lack of focus on what you believe the issue to be.

   *Response:* Eschew jargon, and focus on specifics. Maybe your message isn't getting through because your target is not as familiar with the industry or the project or the product as you. If you find yourself skipping over important details, slow down.

4. *Poor timing:* Sometimes, it's not you; it's the timing. Priorities may be elsewhere. Perhaps it's your firm's busy season, or IT problems in the office are leaving employees distracted and ornery. Or your specific target might just be having a bad day and dealing with issues of which you're completely unaware.

   *Response:* Try to avoid asking for something that directly conflicts with ongoing demands in the first place. (It is ill-advised to swim against the tide, especially a riptide.) However, if you find that you've unwittingly posed an ill-timed request, try practicing reversal. As a high school wrestler, this was one of my specialty moves. Wresting control from my opponents earned me two points each time. In persuasion, it can get you much, much more. Try something like this: "You've got a ton on your plate, I know. That's exactly why we should green-light this project. I can make sure it gets done right and involve you as much or as little as you want. This will prove to the organization that our group is not constrained by capacity."

5. *Opposing self-interest:* This happens when the company, the department, or the individual has a huge economic advantage to do exactly the opposite of what you are pursuing (or to do nothing at all).

   *Response:* This is a tough one, but there are ways to combat it, by appealing to corporate values or long-term benefits. Suggest that your pitch will not create a reversal of goals, and attempt to show your targets how a yes would support their private benefits in the longer term. You also can provide them with a quid pro quo they're not expecting.

6. *X factors:* Stop me if you've heard this one before. Suddenly, an unexpected "expert," such as an outside consultant, weighs in on your pitch. Or an unanticipated development, such as an acquisition or company reorganization, occurs. Or you learn of a personal relationship that could jeopardize your persuasion efficacy, such as the person you thought was in favor of an organizational shift is married to the cousin of the company's general manager.

   *Response:* Damn the torpedoes and keep your persuasion priority moving forward, irrespective of the new information. If that's too bold of a move for you, make sure you have a Plan B. Adjust your ask in light of the new conditions, and try to co-opt new sources of expertise. If you can, change your timing to take advantage of the situation. For example, if a new head of marketing will be announced next week who is charged with taking the target's efforts toward new and younger customers, explain how—with the new hire's guidance—some of your ideas could easily be put into action.

7. *Machiavellian impulses:* I'm referring to the people who tell you one thing (to keep you happy) and then do another (to make them happy). Then they explain their behavior as a misunderstanding (to try to make you happy again). They will take credit for others' work, disassociate themselves from errors of their own, and work behind the scenes to reach their goals—often entering and exiting alliances and friendships in revolving-door fashion.

   *Response:* Machiavellian types also hate the bright light because it exposes their dark corners, so keep issues in the light. Contain them, because it's pointless to fight them, and don't attempt head-on (or headfirst) assaults. Rather, give them the opportunity to (eventually) reveal that the only side they're ever on is their own.

**How to Win an Argument**

The next time you find yourself bracing for an argument, let it go. Why? Because persuasion ends the moment arguing begins. All of a sudden, the objective becomes focused on "winning," and that's when you've already lost.

To prove this point, a group of researchers led by Emory University psychology and psychiatry professor Drew Westen studied functional Magnetic Resonance Imaging (fMRI) of both Democrats and Republicans as they responded to messages from their preferred candidate during the 2004 American presidential election. Specifically, Democrats were shown videos of self-contradictory remarks made by John Kerry, while Republicans were shown self-contradictory remarks from George W. Bush. Both groups of participants tended to dismiss the apparent discrepancies in a manner that demonstrated bias toward their favored candidate.

"Everyone from executives and judges to scientists and politicians may reason to emotionally biased judgments when they have a vested interest in how to interpret 'the facts,'" Westen told the ScienceDaily website after his research was presented in 2006.

When your persuasion attempts reach that point, logic and reason flee your target. Whatever you say after that point of no return will be moot, unless you can steer the conversation back to a rational and legitimate discussion.

So how do you win an argument? Don't let one start.

## 10 EMERGENCY ACTIONS WHEN
## NAVIGATING "ASSENT TURBULENCE"

Fasten your seat belt: Regardless of your attempts to reduce assent turbulence, sometimes you'll get the feeling that your persuasion situation is inexorably heading the wrong way. Professional pilots rate turbulence from Level 1 (light, slightly erratic changes that keep you from enjoying your glass of wine) to Level 4 (extreme, violent motions that convince you you'll never fly again). Your own turbulence will have degrees of intensity as well.

Does someone simply not understand a facet of your request? ("Why do you need two hours at our national sales meeting next month?") This is Level 1 turbulence, which can easily be ameliorated. However, if the CEO received misinformation and, in mafia-speak, "put a contract out on your idea," you're definitely navigating Level 4 turbulence. What to do?

Take the following 10 tips from the pilot's flight manual and see what the pros do when they hit a rough patch of air:

1. *Be calm.* It doesn't help if you, the pilot, are freaked out. Remind yourself that, because this is your priority, you may be amplifying facets of the situation in your mind. Take a deep breath. More than likely, your physical safety isn't in jeopardy, and the fate of the world doesn't hang in the balance.

2. *Switch on the seat belt sign.* Let other passengers know there could be a few bumps. If you're working on that new product training initiative we explored in Chapter 7, you might have any number of people who are aware of your effort and are invested in its success. Let them know there could be, figuratively speaking, some shifting of items in the overhead compartments. Help keep your team calm, too.

3. *Use your radar.* You need to locate and understand the turbulence. Is it thermal, mechanical, or aerodynamic? This is where your networks come into play. You need to have contacts in sales, finance, legal, and other departments—trusted colleagues who understand the importance of sharing information to help you pinpoint the source of the problem.

4. *Subtly test your controls.* Ask for opinions—not comments and certainly not commitments: "Given what you currently know, what are you thinking right now?" Ask about potential storms,

and keep an eye out for someone who can help play the role of problem solver, intermediary, or facilitator.

5. *Level the aircraft.* Always be able to, at any time during the persuasion process, clearly explain what you are trying to initiate, how much it will realistically cost, and what the return will be (and how you will quantify it): "We've covered a lot of territory here. Just so we're clear: Today, we're talking about a purchase order for $225,000 to help our call center talent increase customer satisfaction by a full point in next quarter's satisfaction index report."

6. *Correct the pitch.* Allow yourself to understand your target's hesitation and work to erase invalid preconceptions. Find areas of potential agreement and collaboration, while unearthing resistance that may be unrelated to what you're actually suggesting: "Your concern is related to the project's budget, and I understand that. How about we take a closer look at my proposal and find a middle ground by identifying expenses we could initially forgo?"

7. *Mayday! Mayday! Call a copilot for help.* You may at times need to ask others to have a conversation, offer an opinion, or otherwise help you get the job done. An executive, an expert, or a strategic ally can assist you in thinking through issues. You don't have to fly solo.

8. *Circle the airport.* I don't like to call this tactic stalling; let's think of it as "circling the airport." Sometimes, to be successful, you need to keep an idea alive long enough for the right situation to arise—like a batter fouling off pitches until the perfect one comes along.

9. *Choose a different runway.* We covered the importance of offering options in your pitch in Chapter 7; now you'll need to provide other options to get that pitch back on track: "We can either

select three of these ideas and determine how best to move forward with them, focus on your favorite idea and make that happen, or come up with a new set of ideas."

10. *Abort the destination.* Land somewhere else. Nothing is ever worth "or else." Ancient Greeks preferred to die in battle when they couldn't win, establishing the ultimate example of "or else." Ancient Romans, on the other hand, believed in retreating in the face of overwhelming strength, which gave them the opportunity to fight another day. Be a Roman by leaving doors open and bridges unburned.

## SURVIVING THE TROUGH OF DISILLUSIONMENT

An interesting psychological effect comes into play when you've engaged in a long and difficult persuasion campaign. If you're like many professionals I encounter, you start out enthusiastically on your persuasion campaign with ever-increasing expectations. Then, after some turbulence, you enter a phase I call the "Trough of Disillusionment." This is where you figuratively become battered and bruised and question whether you should even be pursuing your persuasion priority.

My advice? Hang in there! If I've learned one thing in 30 years of working toward yes, it's that the persuasion process sometimes requires tenacity. That said, you do have to know when to say "when." This is where the next idea will help . . .

### The Platinum Rule of Persuasion

I'm often asked how many times someone should attempt to obtain buy-in from a given target before acknowledging rejection. People will tell me that they've just attended some ridiculous sales seminar where they've been told that the "sale doesn't begin until the customer says no." Or that "the customer has to say no six times before you quit." I learned how to sell in a Philadelphia Harley-Davidson dealership. Following that kind of advice would have gotten me punched in the mouth! The advice I use was taught to me from another Philly guy, Joel DeLuca, whom I introduced in Chapter 3. He taught me what I now call the "Platinum Rule of Persuasion," because it works so well: Take two shots, and then salute.

What I mean by this is that if your target says no once, reformulate, and try again. If, after your second attempt, the target's response is still no, salute and move on. (And, as we advised previously, live to persuade another day.) If you hold on to your request with the tenacity of a pit bull locked on to a rump roast, people are going to start saying things to you like, "I like your passion," which, of course, is corporate-speak for, "We think you've lost your mind."

So take two shots, then salute. Say something like, "Thanks for your consideration. I value your input and respect your decision. I'm all the better for having spent time with you on this idea."

## SHOWING GRACE IN THE FACE OF REJECTION

What do you do when your second shot is spent, and you've run out of options? Welcome to the NFL. Let's face it. Over the course of your career, you're going to get rejected more than once. If you're not hearing no at least some of the time, you're probably not stretching yourself enough. That said, how should you respond in that moment of rejection?

- *Don't get angry.* That will just push your target further away.

- *Do show disappointment.* No need to wear a tough poker face after the proposal you spent so much time and energy on gets turned down. As a matter of fact, if you *don't* appear a little disappointed, your target could think your pitch wasn't all that important to you.

- *Do remain respectful.* Use power language when communicating to your target: "Well, of course I'm disappointed. But I'd like to thank you for giving the idea such careful consideration."

In the 1968 movie *The Lion in Winter*—set in England in 1183—
King Henry II has imprisoned his conniving sons, Prince Geoffrey and
Prince Richard, in the wine cellar. When they think they hear their fa-
ther coming down the stairs to kill them, this exchange occurs:

PRINCE RICHARD: He'll get no satisfaction out of me. He isn't going
to see me beg.

PRINCE GEOFFREY: My, you chivalric fool—as if the way one fell
down mattered.

PRINCE RICHARD: When the fall is all that is, it *matters*.

Show grace in the face of rejection.


## BOUNCING BACK FROM NO

If you practice the advice in this book, your batting average will be
much higher than those in the Baseball Hall of Fame. Nevertheless,
you will hear no on occasion, so here are eight ideas to help you bounce
back:

1. *Move on to what's next.* My favorite TV series is the seemingly
   timeless political epic *The West Wing*. In it, Martin Sheen plays
   the role of President Josiah "Jed" Bartlet. It's a terrific program
   that captures a fairly accurate portrayal of life in the White
   House.

   President Bartlet—whether he is triumphant in victory or
   is crushed in defeat—always responds in the same manner:
   "What's next?" What a brilliant example of how to handle any
   situation! Activate the next issue on your agenda, and don't deliberate over defeat. Autopsies are for medical examiners, not
   managers.

2. *Realize that you're not the problem.* In his groundbreaking work
   (which should be required reading for every persuasion profes-

sional), *Learned Optimism: How to Change Your Mind and Your Life* (New York: Vintage Books, 2004), Ph.D. Martin E. P. Seligman notes that optimism won't change what a salesperson says to a prospective buyer; rather, it will change what the salesperson says to himself after a negative exchange. Instead of saying, "I'm no good," he might rationalize that "the client was too busy to fully consider my offer." Furthermore, Seligman maintains that optimism can be learned.

The next time you hear no, take a page from Seligman's playbook and recast the situation thus: Your particular target chose not to agree to your course of action at that particular time. *That's it.* There is no connection to your worth as a person or the validity of your viewpoint.

3. *Understand the external locus of learning.* The idea of learning that you can learn is critical. For individuals who claim that they already know what they need to know, a setback can be devastating. If, on the other hand, you believe your locus of learning is external, you can shrug off the setback and tell yourself, *I'll have to get some coaching or read up on how to improve my presentation skills, so next time I'll experience a better result.* The world always seems a little brighter for these people, because they have more arrows in their quiver.

4. *Ignore unsolicited feedback.* Alan Weiss tells the memorable story of how—following a rousing talk to a capacity crowd that gave him a standing ovation—a speech coach approached him and asked if she could provide some feedback. "Is there anything on the planet that might stop you?" Weiss wisecracked in his own inimitable way. She proceeded to tell him that she couldn't concentrate on his message, because he constantly moved around onstage, and that he should stand still to make a point. The speech coach had other suggestions for him, too.

Pay no attention to suggestions from your so-called supporters—especially if they tell you that you should have tried harder or danced on the ceiling. Instead, seek out constructive feedback from credible individuals you trust.

5. *Perform a self-assessment.* Heed your own counsel. Is this the first rejection you've received regarding your pitch? Or have you been turned down several times making the pitch? Once is an accident, twice is a coincidence, and three times is a pattern. Is a pattern emerging?

6. *Immediately do something you're skilled at doing.* Whether it's writing a memo, coaching a coworker, or giving a talk, go do something at which you know you'll be successful. This success-immediately-after-defeat strategy is a great way to reinstate positive feelings and get them working again in your brain. Even if it's a small victory, it's a victory.

7. *Forget about perfection.* Rather, focus on success direction. Set parameters of success, not either/or outcomes. Think about your results as the volume knob on an amplifier instead of the on/off switch. You turned in a great project and your boss called it "solid" but not "stupendous"? Don't worry about it. Who uses *stupendous* anyway?!

8. *Evaluate your entire body of work.* Hank Aaron had a lifetime batting average of .305; Joe DiMaggio, .325; Ty Cobb, .366; Lou Gehrig, .340; Babe Ruth, .342. These guys failed approximately 7 times out of every 10 trips to the plate. Not only are they in the Baseball Hall of Fame today, their names are woven into the fabric of our language.

   If, when all is said and done, people refer to you as the Joe DiMaggio of New Products, or the Hank Aaron of Project Management, or the Babe Ruth of Marketing—well, you'd be in some pretty solid company. Focus on your whole career, not one or two errors in the field.

### Chapter 9 Persuasion Points

1. Turbulence is inevitable; prepare for it.

2. Unlike a pilot, you can personally prevent (or at least ameliorate) most turbulence around your issue.

3. Some resistance is honest and some is Machiavellian. Understand the distinction and act accordingly.

4. Demonstrate grace and resilience, and never take it personally when you are unsuccessful for the moment.

5. Don't assume you have a problem, but do assess patterns to see if you can improve your future chances.

6. Focus on success, not perfection.

7. Handle surprises with equanimity and don't spring them on others.

8. After hearing no, move on to other aspects of your work and life, and you'll be more effective with your issue in the future.

# Yes Success

## What to Do When Your Target Agrees
## (and Why Most People Don't Get This Right)

We plan for objections and we plan for resistance; but we often don't plan for success. This is a big mistake. Learning to handle this moment with panache will differentiate the Hall of Famers from the also-rans. This is because it is in the moment of yes that you can reassure your target that he or she has made a wise decision. And from there, you can begin to position yourself for even higher levels of persuasion success.

### FIVE MOMENT-OF-YES DON'Ts

When you hear yes, you've accomplished your objective. So don't blow it by falling into one of the following five traps:

1. *Don't immediately reply with an incredulous "Really?"* A response like that can erode any confidence you've already built in your target and have that person second-guessing his decision. You don't want to appear gob-smacked that someone actually believes in your pitch. Sometimes, people seem so shocked at their own success that they inadvertently convey those thoughts to

the target. They feel the need to say something, so they rush to fill the void in the conversation with a silly response.

So what *should* you say? "Excellent." "Fantastic." "Smart move." Even silence is better than a dumbfounded, *"Really?"*

2. *Don't keep trying to make your case.* Just stop.

My first car was a 1967 Dodge Dart, three-speed on a tree. (For you Millennials, that means a manual three-speed shifter on the steering column.) It was far from a new vehicle when I was driving it. If everything wasn't just right, when I attempted to turn off the car the engine would sputter and run and sputter and run some more. Like a cockroach, the Dart wouldn't stop—especially if I was on a date. During those times, I remember cringing with embarrassment and pleading with my Damsel from Detroit, *"Please, just stop!"* That's what your persuaded target will be thinking, too.

3. *Don't review your target's concerns.* Occasionally, you might feel as if there needs to be one final review of all the problems you've solved, and you might be tempted so say something like this: "Okay, so as you know, with the new project time line, we should be able to complete the market analysis before we get the new additions to the field team in place, and before the new finance programs are approved. All of this is dependent on EPA approval of the new system."

Yikes! Your point-by-point review has, all of a sudden, made your target nervous, which might make him renege on his commitment. Don't feel obligated to act as if your target's concerns are top of mind at this point. You've heard those concerns, the target still said yes, and now both of you can move forward.

4. *Don't be unprepared.* You can't anticipate every eventuality, but you can plan for some. If, for example, a purchase order needs to be signed, have it with you and ready to go. If you need to call someone to issue a verbal authorization, have the contact's

name and number programmed into your phone. And for heaven's sake, have a decent pen with you in case you need to write something down. Lack of preparation in the moment of yes could lead your target to second-guess the decision she's just made and bring your credibility into question.

5. *Don't bask in the glow of your success.* When I played baseball as a kid, I was pretty good with the bat. I still vividly remember hitting the ball solidly with my bat's sweet spot and then standing with pride as that ball sailed into the outfield and over the fence. I did this frequently—enough so that my coach would intone, "It doesn't mean anything if you don't run."

   After your target says yes, hit the bases. Simply say, "Excellent. We better get to it." And then start running!

### Why Your Office Is the Ultimate Home-Court Advantage

As many readers know, I consider Robert Cialdini, author of *Influence: The Psychology of Persuasion,* to be the godfather of persuasion. His research, summarized in Chapter 2, laid the groundwork for much of how persuasion is practiced today. One of his studies compared patient compliance with the prescribed behavior dispensed by both physicians and physical therapists. As things turned out, patients followed their doctors' orders, but not their physical therapists'.

When Cialdini evaluated the environments in which the directives were given, he observed that the doctors wore white coats and made their diagnoses and prescriptions in rooms whose walls were adorned with state licenses, medical school diplomas, and other validations of their qualifications. But while the physical therapists themselves possessed equally impressive qualifications, their physical surroundings tended not to tout their credentials, but rather to sport

*(Continued on next page)*

*(Continued from previous page)*

motivational posters (including at least one featuring a kitten, presumably clinging for her life and spouting, "Hang in there!"). Once the posters were replaced with licenses and diplomas, patient compliance increased significantly.

Meaningful credentials speak volumes. Display diplomas, awards, and other documents denoting serious achievement in your work space so targets can clearly see them. Doing so will help your target feel more comfortable about his decision to say yes to you.

## FIVE MOMENT-OF-YES DOs

Just as you can clearly make missteps when you hear yes, there also are actions you can take that will help remove any trace of doubt your target may have left. Here they are:

1. *Immediately shake hands.* I know it seems obvious, but you'd be shocked to realize how many people miss this important moment. Shaking hands is almost always the socially acceptable thing to do (though, in certain cultures, it's a good idea to check—especially in male-to-female agreements) for everything from meeting and greeting to saying thank-you and offering congratulations. A handshake also signals the completion of an agreement. (In the Middle Ages, it also demonstrated that the other person was not holding a concealed weapon!) Even if I've worked with a person for years, on a big agreement, I always shake hands to affirm the commitment.

2. *Offer a reinforcing comment.* While shaking hands, it's critical to also offer some sort of agreement-reinforcing comment: "This is going to be an exciting project." "We will do great work together." "Here's to accomplishing important work." Avoid statements such as "Well, here's hoping it works!" or "Thank you for the opportunity; I hope I make you proud." The objec-

tive here is to fill your target with confidence, not initiate buyer's remorse or demonstrate that your pitching skills are stronger than your confidence.

3. *Give a "next steps" overview.* Here you want to be absolutely clear on what will happen next: "Okay, so I'll work with the legal department this afternoon to put the final details into an agreement. You'll be deciding which budgets to use. And we'll collaborate on the project's announcement this afternoon. By this time tomorrow, we'll be up and running."

   In other words, determine who will handle the purchase order. Who will draft the agreement. Who is communicating what to others. Much like the martial art of aikido, you want to use the natural momentum of the agreement to solidify things and get them moving.

4. *Make sure your target takes action.* In the example above, the target is given next-step responsibilities. That is intentional. Sometimes in the moment of yes, persuaders are so relieved to receive agreement that they take the focus on accountability off the target. Don't create a "sit back and relax" experience for your target. You want her to be required to take action. Your target should be committed to the decision, not merely compliant. The only way that will happen is if she has something to do.

   The balancing act here is in not making that action too onerous. It shouldn't require the cognitive strain of quantum physics or the physical equivalent of shoveling rocks. Suggested activities: Make a phone call, provide a signature, send an email, review a document. Set something you and your target can agree on immediately, then schedule a follow-up session.

5. *Go public.* As I wrote in the beginning of this book, no one wants to be considered a hypocrite. The majority of people want to perform consistently with their publicly stated ideas and positions. So it behooves you to nudge your target to go public. This can take the form of letting just a few people around the lunch

table know about the agreement to distributing a company-wide memo to alerting the local and national media. Going public makes that yes official by naming those accountable and broadcasting the commitment.

## If the Situation Were Reversed . . .

There are moments of extreme power in human exchanges; instances where influence can be wielded for the good of both parties. One of these moments is when someone says, "Thank you." But we often handle these opportunities poorly.

A client thanks you for your help and you say, "No problem. Would have done it for anyone." A coworker thanks you for your assistance and you say, "Sure, it was easy." A supplier sends a note of appreciation and you leave it at that.

Not only are these relationships not furthered, but we may have actually damaged them by these responses. Making someone feel unappreciated, incompetent, or not worthy of a response is a surefire way not to increase your influence.

Another potential problem is when the exchange is framed such that the other party feels they've just done a favor for Vito Corleone ("Someday I may call upon you to do a service for me.") Saying things like, "And now you owe me one" is an excellent way to build animosity and opposition. So how can you avoid making this mistake? Be prepared to use powerful language. That's how. Robert Cialdini, author of the seminal work *Influence: The Psychology of Persuasion*, suggests: "My pleasure, because I know if the situation were reversed, you would have done the same for me!"

Watch as the other person nods furiously in agreement, and you have now used language to expertly and subtly earn a "chit," which is an informal influence credit. Practice this until you can use this (or other similar language) to create compelling yet conversational exchanges.

## CREATING PERPETUAL YES

After the initial joy fades from that long-anticipated moment of yes, you're faced with the aftermath. What now? The key to long-term career success is not just obtaining agreement; it's about obtaining agreement again, and again, and again—creating perpetual yes.

You can do a number of things to ensure this cycle of yes, beginning with the obvious: Perform outstanding work. Nothing gets to yes again and again like past success. As I've reiterated throughout this book, my definition of persuasion is "ethically winning the heart and mind of your target"—not "getting one over" on someone. Persuasion is about allowing your brightest arguments to illuminate the path for others.

Now that you've succeeded with one persuasion priority, get ready to create perpetual yes by understanding how to create, acquire, and leverage testimonials, referrals, and personal persuasion evangelists. A testimonial is static evidence of success (a letter, email, or recording), a referral is someone who comes to you for a particular reason because someone else specifically recommended you, and a personal evangelist is someone who actively sings your praises. You'll need all three if you want to create what I refer to as a "career of perpetual yes."

As shown in Figure 10-1, if you have testimonials and evangelists without referrals, you won't have a pipeline for cool projects and opportunities. If you have referrals and evangelists but no testimonials, you won't have any evidence of your success. If you have testimonials and referrals without evangelists, you'll lack momentum. Build your rock-star career with all three.

### Getting Testimonials

A testimonial is an endorsement of either you or your team. It can speak to character, skill, or result, and it can be a letter, a video, or a voice recording. Even a personal reference counts as a testimonial. I've never met anyone who said testimonials don't matter. Then why don't more people go out and get them? The best persuaders are constantly accumulating testimonials, like trophies, for projects well done.

**Figure 10-1** Creating Perpetual Yes

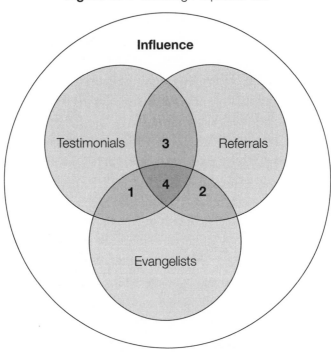

**1** = No pipeline   **2** = No evidence   **3** = No momentum   **4** = Perpetual yes

The best time to capture a testimonial is when that window of opportunity opens. In social exchanges, that might be when someone compliments you or thanks you. Shyness won't help you here. Let's say your happy target shakes your hand, smiles, and says, "You've done a great job on this project. You did everything we talked about and got great results we needed. Thank you!" If you respond with a "Happy to help" or a plain and boring "You're welcome," you're missing a huge opportunity.

You're target is pleased, so now is the time to ask him for a testimonial. He's more likely to say yes now than at any time in the future. But people don't ask, because they don't know how, they consider doing so to be rude, or they fear rejection.

When requesting a testimonial, I suggest something like this: "Happy to help. We're glad the project turned out so well. We're always trying to spread the good news of what we're doing in the sales division. Would you take what you've just told me and put it in a quick email message so I can show others how pleased you are?"

Get testimonials any way you can. I'll take a testimonial via text message, email, voice mail message, or iPhone video. Sometimes, your happy target might even say, "Write something up, and I'll give it a look." Done! Video is most compelling, but I will do whatever the other person prefers in the moment. Don't be bashful about pulling out your camera or phone right there and shooting 30 seconds of spontaneous support! Don't fear rejection, either. You can't walk away with less than you walked in with! You're simply trying to create leverage to further your goals.

The greatest aspect of testimonials is that they can be used all the time, with both internal and external clients, buyers, and targets. Drop them into conversation with others: "This project is important, and we're confident about our projections. I know you know Anne Emerich in product development. We worked with her on a big project last quarter. She used the word *astonished* when she described how close our projected return matched the projection."

Pull pithy quotes and add them to your email signature, too—"the best marketer in Dallas!"—and provide references to them in your proposal cover letters and other materials.

### Leveraging Referrals

While testimonials are static statements for a job well done, a referral is an introduction to another potential client or customer. One person says to another, "You should really talk to Tom. He did terrific work on our project, and he might be able to help you."

The next best thing to someone witnessing your outstanding performance is having a trusted colleague tell someone else about that outstanding performance. Call them referrals, call them introductions, call them networking opportunities. Whatever. Just *take advantage* of them.

Referrals will help your persuasion efforts because they provide your target with a "warm" contact. You're a friend of a friend, a welcome visitor, a known entity. This offers instant credibility and removes the time and effort required to "prove" yourself and your credentials or ideas. Your target is immediately and seamlessly involved.

Yet, like getting testimonials, many people don't leverage referrals. I call it "referral reluctance." They don't want to imperil a new relationship and are more concerned with being liked than being respected, with gaining affiliation instead of gaining an objective. They also don't want to sound like a salesperson. They feel, inexplicably, that they are asking for something instead of contributing something, trying to take instead of give. Sometimes, people feel as though they will put the other person in an awkward position. In those cases, their sympathy outweighs their empathy.

In addition, there exists a phenomenon called "referral deferral," whereby your persuaded target doesn't want to sound as though he is pushing your business toward others. In some cases, that target may have been "burned" before when making what turned out to be a bad referral to a friend. Or perhaps, people don't like when they are put in a similar position. Other possible reasons for referral deferral include not wanting others to think they are part of a manipulative action, not knowing what to say, lacking trust, or simply possessing an innate cynicism that precludes them from reaching out to colleagues and peers.

You can help overcome referral reluctance and deferral by establishing a good rapport early on. Securing referrals and introductions shouldn't be an ambush. So, if you're working with someone on a project and think you'd like to leverage that person for future referrals and introductions, simply say something like, "My objective is to make you so deliriously happy that you'll want to tell others about our great work." This will make you memorable, because a lot of people don't make such bold statements. "Deliriously happy" is compelling language, like Babe Ruth calling his shot.

I like to end such conversations with a quick confirming question: "Fair enough?" "Sound good?" Now your target has gone on record and will be more inclined to follow through on that referral, because he promised he would.

**Obtaining Referrals in the First Place.** Timing, in business and just about anything else, is everything. Some moments are better than others when asking for a referral. You don't want to ask too early in the project, because you may not have delivered or begun to show results yet. That would be like proposing marriage on the first date. You also don't want to wait too long, because, no matter how well you've performed on an assignment, enthusiasm cools and memory fades.

The two best times?

1. *When your target has made a significant, mid-project positive comment.* For instance: "Working with you is so easy!" Now, *that* is an opportune time, because I have never seen a project go smoothly the entire time. There always seems to be a midcourse correction required or a misunderstanding or an argument at some point during the process. So take advantage of propitious moments when you can.

2. *When your target has indicated excitement and you sense you can capitalize on it.* This might be during your project wrap-up, while reviewing positive results, or whenever you hear such trigger terms as "excellent," "pleased," "satisfied," "terrific," and the ever-popular "awesome" and "amazing."

Again, as with testimonials, asking for referrals requires charm and savvy: "We're thrilled you're so pleased with the way things went. Remember, our goal was to make you deliriously happy. Who else in the organization could you recommend who might benefit from working with us?" (Here is where terms like "recommend," "suggest," and "advise" really pay off.)

**Maintaining the Referral Relationship.** After receiving a referral, don't overlook the importance of following up with the referring party. Always keep that person in the loop. That way, he or she can help if the third party isn't immediately responsive. This will additionally motivate the referrer to provide you with more contacts and support. After all, the referring party will score some points with his or her sources, too.

### Creating Personal Evangelists

An evangelist, of course, is someone who promulgates something enthusiastically. There already exist religion evangelists, technology evangelists, and brand evangelists. Now I'm suggesting you create personal evangelists: people who sing your praises and attempt to convert others to, well, you. Here are five ways to do just that:

1. *Be a rebel with a cause.* In a research paper published in the *Journal of Consumer Research*, Caleb Warren and Margaret C. Campbell define *cool* as: "a subjective, positive trait perceived in people, brands, products, and trends that are autonomous in an appropriate way." The researchers cited a 1984 Apple advertisement as a prime example. In essence, it communicated that "You have a choice" and then implored "Don't buy IBM." Note: The ad didn't say, "Burn IBM's headquarters to the ground." So be "out there"—but with boundaries.

2. *Don't try to appeal to everyone.* If you want true staying power, you can't appeal to everyone. Yep. You read that right. The rock band KISS, an ongoing entity for more than 40 years, with some 80 million albums sold, was inducted into the Rock and Roll Hall of Fame in 2014. One of the main reasons the band made it that far is because it created a rabid group of evangelists known as the KISS Army, which packed tremendous staying power. These people are devoted fans. Lead vocalist Paul Stanley said it best: "Either love us or hate us. If you're in the middle, get out."

3. *Take care of those who support you.* Lessons also can be learned from another rock band, albeit one with a much different musical style than KISS. The Grateful Dead's evangelists, known collectively as "Deadheads," demonstrate the power of the people in almost everything they do. For example, while the Grateful Dead buck convention in many ways, it's still shocking to think that the band has allowed Deadheads to record their shows for free and actively encouraged bootlegging of their music for decades. Why? Because it endears the band to the fans. Reciprocity, anyone? (I'd love to see Justin Bieber's management team pitch that idea. Or, for that matter, KISS.)

4. *Be elegant.* Steve Jobs was so fanatical about design that he added costs and increased development time by raving about the importance of the aesthetic design of the circuitry found *inside* Apple products. Everything you do should be as elegant as the circuitry in your MacBook Air. Earlier, we covered the importance of creating sartorial persuasion by dressing sharply and pulling your office together—both of which can do big things for your persuasion powers. Now apply that approach to emails you send, documents you create, and PowerPoint presentations you deliver. Make sure everything has what graphic designers used to call "eye-wash": Your stuff not only has to *be* good; it has to look good, too.

5. *Be like Billy.* And speaking of speaking, I mean speak like *actual* evangelist Billy Graham. I asked a person whose opinion I respected who was the greatest speaker he'd ever heard? His reply: "Billy Graham. And I'm agnostic!"

   Speaking is one of the most effective ways to create personal evangelists. Know your topic, engage your crowd, and deliver your message with enthusiasm. Whether you should mimic Billy Graham's style or content is up for debate, but exceptional speaking skills can create a tent-revival atmosphere around you and your persuasion priorities.

If you really want your career to race toward success like a Top Fuel dragster, you need to carefully prepare for success.

---

### Chapter 10 Persuasion Points

1. Be prepared to exploit success when people agree.

2. Know when to stop "selling" and begin "sowing."

3. Use language to propel discussions and actions.

4. Exude confidence and enthusiasm, both of which are infectious.

5. Nothing gets to yes again and again like past success.

6. Never fail to seek testimonials and referrals.

7. Find ways to overcome "referral reluctance" and "referral deferral."

8. Choreograph, orchestrate, and set the stage to hear perpetual yes.

# Your Persuasion Action Plan

## How to Get a 10,000:1 Return on Your Investment in This Book

I know what you're thinking: *A 10,000:1 ROI is an outrageous claim!* (After all, you read Chapter 4, so you've mastered ROI calculations.) Okay, since you brought it up, let's do the math.

If you paid $25 for this book, then $250,000 would get you in the ballpark of a 10,000:1 financial return. For a typical consultant, that would be comparable to securing five $50,000 contracts. A salesperson earning 15 percent commission would need to sell approximately $1.65 million worth of goods or services. A salaried person working for a corporation could realize that kind of return by jumping from a $100,000-a-year job to a $150,000-a-year job in a few short years.

All of these scenarios are well within the realm of possibility. But you *need to apply the ideas*—or all bets are off. You also need to be willing to take some chances, so consider this: *What are you willing to do to make it?*

In the August 31, 1972, East Coast edition of *Rolling Stone* magazine, an unknown musician named Peter Criscuola ran an ad that read:

"Drummer: willing to do anything to make it." Two guys looking to create a band, Stanley Eisen and Gene Klein, called Peter to explore his seriousness. "Would you wear a dress onstage?" he asked. "Would you wear high heels?" "Would you wear . . . makeup?"

And the rest, as they say, is KISStory.

Peter Criscuola became Peter Criss; Stanley Eisen became Paul Stanley; and Gene Klein became Gene Simmons. The trio quickly added guitarist Ace Frehley, and the rock band KISS eventually wound up in the Rock and Roll Hall of Fame. Perhaps the story of the band's origins is apocryphal—but if it didn't happen, it should have.

I'm not suggesting you dress like your favorite member of KISS on casual Friday, but those guys were willing to go beyond the norm and define new parameters for rock music and performance in the face of early ridicule. So what is your answer? *What are you willing to do to make it?*

## POWERING THROUGH UNCERTAINTY

You may remember that we discussed cognitive biases in Chapter 2. As you well know, they are always in play—affecting our thoughts and actions, as well as those of our targets. And when it comes to taking action, one bias is particularly insidious—the certainty illusion, which is sometimes described as "the unreasonable desire for 100 percent confidence or certainty." Yet few aspects of life are certain. We can't be certain that a doctor's prognosis is correct, that voting machines are infallible, that the Green Bay Packers will win the Super Bowl. This, however, shouldn't stop us from getting the physical exam, doing our civic duty, or watching the Packers-Bears game on Monday night.

On page 11, I asked you to define your persuasion priority. Now, we're going to do more than just consider the issues; we're going to jump in the pool and start making some waves—*which means taking deliberate, purposeful action*. So let's examine your persuasion priority from two perspectives: risk and result.

## Taking No Risk

Peek ahead to Figure 11-1 on page 195. This is going to be the object of our discussion for the foreseeable future. This figure has a number of distinguishing features, and we'll discuss each in turn. For the time being let's focus on the risk continuum scale—the x axis that spans from Foolish Risk on the left to Calculated Risk on the right.

The risk continuum scale should look somewhat familiar to you from the figures in the first few chapters, but this one is articulated by numbers, because in this situation it's important to think of your actions and results in terms of degrees, not just black-and-white conditions. Not pursuing a priority connotes no risk. Consequently, it is represented by the 0 in the center of the risk continuum scale. Every step away from the center moves increasingly toward either a negative or a positive risk.

## Moving Toward a Foolish Risk

The degree of foolish risk depends on how far to the left you move on the continuum.

-1: Making an out-of-the-blue ask of a friendly target: "Jim, how about if you let me craft the proposal?"

-2: Making a significant out-of-the-blue ask of a friendly target: "Jim, would you like me to make the client presentation?"

-3: Making a significant request, with little case building, of a negative target: "Steve, I know we haven't always seen eye-to-eye, but I have a gut feeling that this is the way to go."

-4: Making a significant request, with little case building, of a negative target group: "Look, Steve, I know this executive group has turned us down before, but I really think we have a winner with this product."

-5: Making an insistent, emotional plea to senior management with no proof or evidence: "I know you're the CEO, but you have to listen to me. This is what's going to happen. I can feel it."

## Moving Toward a Calculated Risk

The degree of calculated risk depends on how far to the right you move on the continuum.

+1: Planting the seed for a reasonable new request of a friendly target: "Jim, I'd love to broaden my skill set. Maybe sometime you could teach me how to put together a winning proposal."

+2: Making a reasonable new request of a friendly target: "Jim, would you like me to have a go at writing the proposal, and you can critique it?"

+3: Making a significant request, with solid case building, of a negative target: "Steve, I know we haven't always seen eye-to-eye, but I'd like to start fresh. Your team and I have put together some numbers on the new project, and it might have some merit. Would you be willing to let us know what you think?"

+4: Making a significant request, with solid case building, of a negative target group: "Look, Steve, we've done our homework for this project and anticipated every possible objection and rebuttal that could come our way. It's gonna work."

+5: Making a well-constructed, well-substantiated case to senior management: "We've analyzed this quantitatively, we've attempted to evaluate this qualitatively, and we've tested this position from three different viewpoints. We think it's a solid proposal."

## Yielding No Result

Now let's take another peek at Figure 11-1 and talk about results. If there is no payoff for you, that would be represented by a 0 on the y axis—meaning you are status quo. Have you ever expended a tremendous effort on a project and gotten nowhere with it? That's what we're talking about here.

At the extremes along the y axis, we have "Breakthrough" and "Breakdown." Moving toward a breakthrough indicates you're on an upward (positive) trajectory, while a "breakdown" suggests you're starting to lose credibility or your persuasion panache. Let's look at the degrees in between.

### Heading for a Breakdown

The degree of breakdown depends on how close to the bottom you move on the scale.

- −1: Mild embarrassment in front of a coworker and some time wasted: "Mike, I read your proposal. There are several miscalculations in it."

- −2: Mild embarrassment in front of a group of colleagues and significant time wasted: "Hey, Mike. The team looked through your slide deck. We can't let you go to the client with *this* presentation."

- −3: A setback in front of your boss: "Sally, we know you've been working with Mike, but this report just won't cut it."

- −4: A setback in front of your boss's boss: "Who hired this guy?"

- −5: Failure, resulting in significant financial loss, legal action, and reputation damage: "Mike, we lost the business, the client has filed suit, you're named as a defendant, and they're profiling our failure on *60 Minutes*."

### Heading Toward a Breakthrough

The degree of breakthrough depends on how close to the top you move on the scale.

- +1: You'll feel good about your accomplishment: "Hey, I did pretty well running the numbers on the project."

+2: Others in your group will notice your accomplishment: "That was a very compelling presentation!"

+3: Your boss will formally acknowledge your win: "Stephanie, I want to thank you. You did a great job bringing aboard that client."

+4: You'll experience an increase in compensation and repute: "Stephanie, as a result of your success, I'm issuing you a new title and a new salary grade."

+5. This will be a game changer for you and your organization: "Stephanie, that project will make us number one in market share, thanks to you. That's why I'm appointing you senior VP and naming the west corner meeting room after you."

As stated earlier, you might choose different descriptors for your estimation of risks and results, but it is important to consider both. Now, when we cross-reference both of these conditions, the full picture of your persuasion possibilities comes together.

### Navigating the Four Quadrants with Intention

Figure 11-1 depicts what I call "decision quadrants." This model can help you think through your efforts in advance and help you decide whether you want to move forward with your actions. Generally speaking, the farther your score is from center, the more intense the sentiment. Think of this as the volume buttons on your iPhone.

If you find yourself in the lower-left quadrant, what I call the area of "Unequivocally 'No!'" for example, the pain of "no" will be tough to recover from. I call the lower-right quadrant "Definitely 'Maybe.'" It's a calculated risk, and you've got a shot, but the payoff isn't overwhelming. So why is it "Definitely 'Maybe'"? Because it might give you exposure to a new person, or it might give you a "live fire" opportunity to practice a new skill, such as making a presentation or running the

**Figure 11-1**  Decision Quadrants

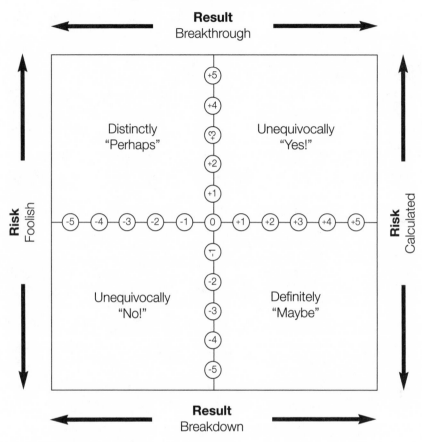

numbers. So, although there may not be a meaningful enough return, you still might receive some benefit. Remember the breakdown scale states –1 through –4 as mild embarrassment to a setback. Sometimes you have to break down before you break through.

The upper-left quadrant, "Distinctly 'Perhaps,'" combines the more dangerous side of the risk scale with the more appealing side of the result scale. That's why actions here require careful consideration. Let's say you receive a phone call notifying you of an impromptu meeting with senior managers to discuss specific aspects of a new product launch. The meeting is in one hour, and you have a great idea for the marketing campaign that you've been thinking about pitching. Perhaps it's not yet crystallized, or you haven't organized your case as well as you'd like, or thought through every aspect of your request, and now there's no time to generate hard numbers. But at this meeting, you may have a shot at making your request. Should you take it? Welcome to the game!

The upper-right is the easiest quadrant to discover you're in. The payoff is on the positive end of the result continuum, approaching "Breakthrough," and despite the risk, you like your chances. This is the quadrant of "Unequivocally 'Yes!'" And the bigger the payoff and the more calculated the risk, the higher your intensity should be to pursue this priority.

If you're convinced you're engaged in a worthy cause with reasonable risk and positive reward, its time to create your Persuasion Action Plan.

## YOUR SEVEN-STEP PERSUASION ACTION PLAN

By now, you should be familiar with the basic elements of your Persuasion Action Plan—you just don't realize it yet. However, in Chapter 1 you learned how to clearly state *who* is the one person you want to do *what* as well as how to determine *why* this is important for you, your target, and your organization. In Chapter 3 (and a bit in Chapter 4) you learned how to assess your primary target and other key influencers. In Chapter 4 you learned how to build your quantitative and qualitative case. In Chapter 6 you learned how to plan your language (by deliberately using adjectives, metaphors, examples, stories, humor, and so forth). In Chapter 7 you learned how to create your action steps. And in Chapter 8 you learned how to map the persuasion territory. Now it's time to put all those skills together and create your own, personalized step-by-step Persuasion Action Plan that fast-tracks you on the road to yes!

## Step 1: Set Your Persuasion Priority

Clearly state *who* is the one person you want to do *what*. Keep in mind the four persuasion priority criteria: Your ask must be meaningful, significant, realistic, and others-oriented. And it *must* be specific. (Reminder: Don't say: "I want my senior vice president to add some people to my staff sometime." Instead say: "I would like my senior vice president to approve five key new hires for my department by the start of next quarter.")

Now it's your turn: *Who* do you want to do *what*?

I want _____ to _____

_____

_____ .


## Step 2: Articulate Why This Priority Is Important to You, Your Target, and Your Organization

Strive to identify at least three reasons for each of the three categories. These can include finances gained, skills acquired, networks built, market shares increased, reputations improved, and others.

Important to you: _____

Important to your target: _____

Important to your company: _____


## Step 3: Build Your Quantitative and Qualitative Cases

When building your quantitative case, you'll want to articulate the anticipated Return on Investment (expressed in dollars, as a percentage, or as a ratio). If you're strategizing a larger and longer-term project, what might be the Net Present Value and the Internal Rate of Return? What other benefits of achieving this priority can be readily quantified?

When building your qualitative case, you want to ask questions such as: Will your initiative result in sustained high morale (and how might you know)? Will the initiative lead to more effective teamwork? (If so, what might be the evidence?) What other qualitative reasons (and subsequent evidence) can you add?

## Step 4: Plan Your Language

What savvy phrases can you use to describe your request or facets of your request? (You might describe "a *compelling* argument, a *sensitive* situation, a *crucial* decision," for instance.) Questions work, too: "Do we want to *surrender* to the competition?"

What figures of speech (metaphor, simile, analogy) can you create to describe your request or subsequent risks or rewards? "This guy is the Peyton Manning of sales directors." "That part of the country is a marketing black hole." "The likelihood of the board approving that approach is less than that of Lady Gaga wearing a turtleneck tomorrow."

Using the power of storytelling, develop a brief and relatable story to justify your request, address potential challenges, or describe imminent rewards. Be sure your story has a purpose, includes a captivating open, establishes a plot, inserts an unexpected element or a couple of humorous comments, and concludes with a learning point.

Anticipate resistance and objection. How will you respond when someone says, "It costs too much"? Or, "We don't need it"? Or, "Now is not the right time"?

## Step 5: Assess Your Primary Target and Other Key Players

You certainly don't need to list every person who might be involved in your request, but it's critical to evaluate your primary target and the key players. Write down their names and titles, your impression of their personalities, and your perception of their preferences for communication and information. For example: "Steve Miller, VP Field Operations; Expressive; text messages; just the facts." Or: "Sandra Mathers, General Counsel, Analytical; face-to-face; all the details."

## Step 6: Map the Political Territory

If your persuasion priority involves more than a few people, represents significant dollars, and is likely to take some time, you should map the political territory. Using the information covered about this technique in Chapter 8, answer five basic questions:

1. Who are the key players?

2. On a scale of $-10$ to $+10$, what is each player's influence in the organization?

3. On a scale of $-10$ to $+10$, to what extent is each player applying that influence in this situation?

4. What are the chances (low, medium, or high) that each player might change his or her position?

5. What significant relationships exist among key players?

Use the information culled from the previous five questions to create a data sheet, and then map your political territory like we did in Chapter 8.

## Step 7: Launch the Five-Step Persuasion Process

By this point, you have thoroughly evaluated your risk and reward, as well as determined whether you'd like to move forward with your persuasion priority. You've articulated your request, and identified not only your self-interest, but also the enlightened self-interest of others. You've crafted your case, crunched the numbers, created compelling language, and counted on and counteracted any resistance. You've identified the key players in your request, considered their personalities and preferences, and mapped your persuasion terrain. Now you're ready to launch the five-step persuasion process (introduced in Chapter 7) that will take you to your objective. Remember the magic formula: $E^2F^3$? To recap:

*Step 1:* Engage your target on the topic; ask for his or her input.

*Step 2:* Explore the issues—with your target and others. Brainstorm options, run numbers and different scenarios, and so forth.

*Step 3:* Form and frame options to get your desired result.

*Step 4:* Finesse any white water and ask for your target's opinion.

*Step 5:* Finalize and formalize the decision—and create perpetual yes.

While engaged in this process, make sure you avail yourself of all the ideas we've talked about on the previous pages. Of course, you won't use all the tools and techniques all at once. Just as a surgeon carefully selects his blade or a golfer her club, your skill and ability to choose and use these techniques will determine your success.

The classic model for the persuasive process has five steps, as defined above. However, each situation is unique, and this model is meant to be flexible. So create as many action steps as is helpful and necessary for the foreseeable future. (For instance, you might want to meet with the financial analyst to see if the numbers make sense before proceeding to the official "Step 1.") However, don't make your sequence overly complicated. You probably don't need 27 action steps, but 2 might be too few. You can then adjust accordingly as your persuasion campaign develops.

Why do you think NFL coaches script as many as the first 15 plays they plan to run? To test the waters and gauge how opponents react, of course, as well as to determine if there are weaknesses, such as a poor pass defense, that can be exploited. Just like coaching, persuading is an art form, and it takes time to master.

To ensure that you fully think through each of your action steps, try implementing the "what, when, why, and how approach." For instance, if you *do* decide that you need to review the numbers with the financial analyst before proceeding to the official "Step 1," you might articulate your goals for this as follows:

*What:* Approach financial analyst Corey Williamson and ask for ROI estimate input.

*When:* Before COB next Friday.

*Why:* We have a great relationship, so he'll be honest with me when evaluating both pros and cons. Presenting a solid financial case will show I'm serious. Plus, if this idea doesn't prove to have a great ROI for the company, I shouldn't move forward.

*How:* Corey is at his best in the morning. He's also a text message guy who hates surprises and loves details. I'll send a text, set up an A.M. meeting, and bring all the details for his perusal.

Try scripting the five steps in your persuasion process in this manner and see what develops.

## THE PAYOFF OF PLANNING

When I present persuasion this way, more than one person usually asks me, "Do I *really* need to do all this? Can't I just go pitch it?" Sure, you can. It all depends on how big your ask is and how important the result is to you and your organization. You certainly wouldn't unleash your Seven-Step Persuasion Action Plan horsepower when trying to persuade someone to go to a seafood restaurant for lunch. But if you're vying for that coveted assignment, looking to add significant numbers to your staff, or pitching your board of directors on a new strategic initiative, you better be on top of your game.

The rule of thumb is that planning pays off in a 5:1 ratio. Every hour you spend planning pays off by saving you roughly five hours of misdirected effort. So do the planning work up front and save the execution headache later.

As you can tell from my tone throughout this book, it's important to have a sense of humor about persuasion. Yet, at the same time, these are seriously powerful approaches for people who are serious about success. If you fit this description, I have just one question before this chapter's Persuasion Points:

*What are you willing to do to make it?*

---

### Chapter 11 Persuasion Points

1. Relentlessly seek opportunities to take calculated risk for breakthrough results.

2. Always consider the environment of your organization or setting when determining your Persuasion Action Plan.

3. Evaluating the risks and potential results of your persuasion priority allows you to take deliberate and purposeful action.

4. Scripting your five-step persuasion process will help you better develop and perfect your pitch.

5. Just like coaching football, persuading is an art form, and it takes time to master.

6. A sense of humor can pay off during the persuasion process.

# The Psychology of Self-Persuasion

### The First Person Who Needs to Say Yes . . . Is You

*I can't apply for that position,* thought the thirtysomething product quality manager engineer. *I'll never get it.*

Some people squeeze stress balls when they think through things. Tom Butler had a baseball. And not just any baseball, but a limited-edition 2004 Boston Red Sox World Series commemorative ball. He rotated it in his hand, the way a reliever might in the late innings of a crucial game. He clicked back over to his Microsoft Outlook and hit the send/receive button. More emails. As he scanned the seemingly endless list of meeting invites, CYA cc's, and the occasional offering for a Russian bride that slipped through the spam filters, his mind kept wandering back to the new job posting he saw earlier that morning. He quickly tiled his windows and went back to the intranet job-posting page.

The enticing link stared back at the young multitasker. He clicked it—for the 11th time—and once again read through the job description: Director of New Product Engineering > fast-paced work environment; must be skilled at managing others; bring keys to future company growth.

Tom's thoughts bounced back and forth like a tennis volley on Wimbledon's Centre Court. *I'd be perfect for that spot.* And behind that thought, with the speed and intensity of a Serena Williams backhand, *But I can't apply. I'm lucky to have* this *job.*

\* \* \*

## WHEN TALKING TO YOURSELF IS A GOOD THING

Whether it's chasing a new job, requesting a plum assignment, or making a budget pitch to the board of directors, we all talk to ourselves before we take action. Many psychologists have labeled this ongoing mental dialogue "self-talk." These internal comments impact thoughts, emotions, actions, and ultimately careers and life itself. The following quote, attributed to everyone from Mahatma Gandhi to Ralph Waldo Emerson to the president of a leading supermarket chain, illustrates this cause and effect:

Watch your thoughts, they become words;

Watch your words, they become actions;

Watch your actions, they become habits;

Watch your habits, they become your character;

Watch your character, for it becomes your destiny.

The point is made even more elegantly in one of my all-time favorite books, *As a Man Thinketh* by philosopher James Allen, published just after the turn of the 20th century (New York: Barse & Hopkins) and reprinted many times. It may very well have been the first "self-help" book. "Man is made or unmade by himself; in the armory of thought he forges the weapons by which he destroys himself," Allen wrote. "He also fashions the tools with which he builds for himself heavenly mansions of joy and strength and peace."

What are *you* building?

## AVOIDING UNPRODUCTIVE SELF-DOUBT

Allen addressed the curious phenomenon of self-talk. If left unchecked, those thoughts often skew negative. "A man's mind may be likened to a garden, which may be intelligently cultivated or allowed to run wild," he wrote. Negative self-talk can be disastrous for your persuasion attempts. That's why this chapter will guide you through common professional persuasion challenges by teaching you to cope with the vicissitudes of professional life. It is *not* intended to be used for medical or psychiatric purposes.

### Analyzing Self-Doubt

In some cultures, self-doubt carries the same type of stigma as leprosy in biblical times, polio in the early 20th century, and HIV/AIDS in the 1980s. That's why you hear some people brag, "I never doubt myself!" There's a word for that kind of thinking: *denial*. We *all* experience self-doubt, in one form or another, whether we want to admit it or not. And this is, in some ways, a good thing: More than likely, self-doubt is a mental condition hardwired in man's prehistoric brain, and it likely was one of the things that kept *Australopithecus africanus* alive on the Serengeti Plains. ("I don't think I can kill that saber-toothed tiger with just this stick.")

For modern-day *Homo sapiens*, however, self-doubt sounds more like, "I can't possibly apply for that job." Today, self-doubt is often what keeps you from yes success. This, too, has a name: the "impostor phenomenon."

In 1985, psychologist Pauline Rose Clance published a book called *The Impostor Phenomenon: Overcoming the Fear That Haunts Your Success* (Atlanta, GA: Peachtree Publishers), in which she describes how highly successful people battle inferiority. Successful executives, professional athletes, and celebrities all at one time or another believe someone will find out they aren't as good as everybody thinks they are. In other words, they're unable to internalize their success and accomplishments. This mental condition hinders talent and contributions. You, too, may have experienced the impostor syndrome. For instance, if you know you're good at number crunching but walk around on eggshells as if someone's about to play the ace, you're experiencing the impostor syndrome. Clance estimates that 70 percent of all people have an impostor syndrome.

Regardless of what you call it, self-doubt manifests itself in many ways. Here are some examples of what self-doubt looks like in the workplace:

- You don't apply for the open position.

- You don't make the pitch.

- You don't ask for help when you need it.

- You don't request a customer testimonial.

- You don't solicit your manager's recommendation.

- You don't request the sales referral.

Similarly, mental self-flagellation is a not-so-distant cousin of self-doubt. This is when you chastise yourself for screwing up a report or questioning why you didn't present the statistics before you shared your opinions in the board meeting. And this internal pattern can destroy self-esteem. In fact, it can be such an insidious habit that psychologist Eugene Sagan labeled the phenomenon as having a "pathological critic." Whether your own pathological critic took up residence in your head during your early years or later in your professional life doesn't matter. Either way, if this line of thinking sounds familiar, you have your own mental drill sergeant to deal with on a daily basis.

## Self-Doubt and Persuasion

All of these manifestations of self-doubt can become problematic for your persuasion efforts. Why? Because persuasion is about taking risks. Because it requires you to put yourself "out there" by taking a stance and asking for agreement. Because persuasion is mostly about taking action, not sitting back hoping the action will occur on account of someone else's effort. And because self-doubt can paralyze you.

And this, my friend, is a serious problem!

You want to become a master of persuasion. (After all, that *is* why you bought this book in the first place, right? I presume you didn't, say, need a doorstopper.) Well then. This is the part of the book where you need to commit to take charge of your thoughts. "Mental toughness is essential to success," Vince Lombardi once said. He should know: He led the Packers to victories in the first two Super Bowls. And just as Lombardi coached his players to train their physiques to win football championships, you can train your mind to win persuasion championships.

One way to train a champion mind is by understanding the interrelatedness and importance of self-esteem, self-efficacy, and self-confidence. These words are, of course, familiar to us all. But to be empowered to put these ideas into action, we need to really understand the concepts. So let's briefly review each in turn.

*Self-esteem* can be defined as one's opinion of oneself as a person, the pride you have in yourself, or your self-respect. The term has evolved over time—with various people emphasizing certain facets. Matthew McKay and Patrick Fanning, in their book *Self-Esteem: A Proven Program of Cognitive Techniques for Assessing, Improving, and Maintaining Your Self-Esteem* (3rd Ed. Oakland, CA: New Harbinger Publications, 2000) (first published in 1987), describe self-esteem as the emotional *sine qua non* (an essential condition); consultant Alan Weiss, who has done tremendous work in the area of self-esteem, describes the word as a verb—an action that leads to self-confidence; and I consider self-esteem a necessary mental condition that allows you to acquire the skills required to persuade. Think of it as your persuasion foundation.

*Self-efficacy* is a person's belief in his or her capabilities to perform a particular task or in the ability to *acquire* the necessary skills to perform that task. Or, as I like to define the term, "having the grit, spit, and determination to get things done." Can you make a compelling presentation? Can you calculate a Net Present Value and discuss its relevance? Can you demonstrate the perseverance to study for a master's degree while working full time? If you can, you've proven your self-efficacy.

*Self-confidence* means demonstrating a general sense that you will be successful. Be careful here, though, as the line between confidence and cockiness is paved with peril. For me, confidence is best displayed by the assuredness that you will be able to accomplish a task. Whether it's winning the business, meeting the deadline, or smoothing the ruffled feathers of a relationship gone awry, you have the capacity to maintain the cool demeanor to get the job done.

Put them all together and . . . Bang!

## The Big Bang Theory of the Psychology of Self-Persuasion

Some people's opinions may differ, but what I see most often in my work is that self-esteem results in self-efficacy, self-efficacy breeds self-confidence, and self-confidence leads to persuasion success. I call this the "Big Bang Theory of the Psychology of Self-Persuasion."

In other words, if you think of yourself as talented and capable, you'll work to learn new skills, such as how to calculate Internal Rate of Return. When you acquire that skill set, you'll be more confident in speaking with influential others in project meetings. And when you're more confident in those meetings, you'll be more inclined to make an effort to gain support for your persuasion priorities. See how this works? For an even clearer perspective, refer to Figure 12-1.

The reverse of these events, however, can also be true—and be catastrophic. If your self-esteem is either partially or wholly dependent on your persuasion success (winning that promotion or prevailing in an argument), be prepared for the psychological equivalent of a black hole. The gravity of your situation will not even allow light to shine through. Imagine the devastating effect this could have on your career.

Here is an example of how everything can go downhill if you rely on positive feedback to boost your self-esteem: Let's say you don't un-

**Figure 12-1** Persuasion Psychology Big Bang Theory

derstand what people are talking about when it comes to finances. You asked a question once in a meeting, and several people laughed at your lack of financial acumen. Subsequently, you withdraw whenever financial matters are discussed. You don't participate, and you feel as if you don't really belong at meetings with people of this caliber. Figure 12-2 shows what this paralyzing dynamic looks like.

**Figure 12-2** Persuasion Psychology Black Hole

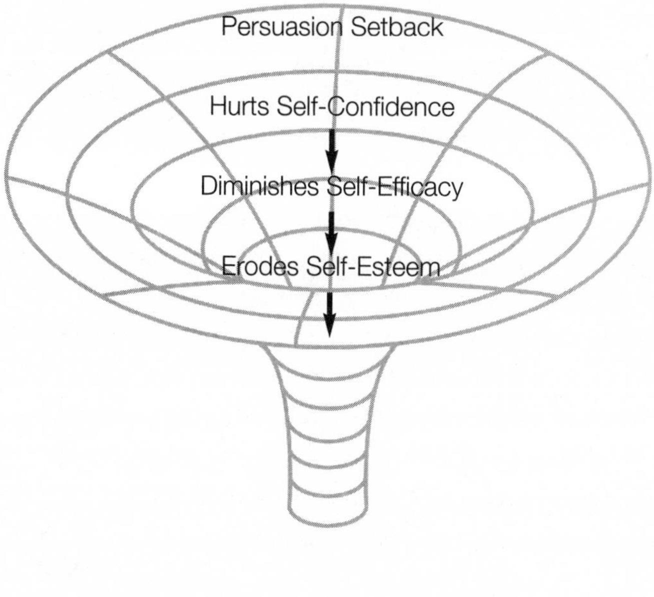

This is a soul-crushing, potentially career-destroying, psychological state. The biggest problem in this dynamic is that you've handed over your mental wellness to the feedback and criticism of others. So the question is: Do you have to do good to be good? Excluding the theological perspective, which is beyond the scope of this book, no—you don't. You have worth and value *despite* what happened at yesterday's staff meeting. To be honest, though, if you aren't so good at something, how do you build the self-esteem to make the effort to be good at it? How can you have more big bangs and fewer black holes?

## DEVELOPING WEAPONS-GRADE SELF-CONFIDENCE

Living with low self-esteem, debilitating self-efficacy, and declining self-confidence steals your energy and ability to cope with anxiety, problems, challenges, and risks. That's the bad news. The good news is that attaining that high self-esteem, solid self-efficacy, and weapons-grade self-confidence does exactly the opposite. It enables you to solve problems rather than worry about them, find ways to win people over, and work directly and purposefully to find solutions.

Many of the following ideas could fall under a category of psychology referred to as "cognitive therapy"—that is, participating in activities, exercises, and conversations that improve your "self-talk," or ongoing internal dialogue, and therefore impact everything from your emotional state to your persuasive performance. For some, this is the purview of incense-burning, beard-wearing, New Age types who wouldn't be caught dead without their yoga mats. If you have that bias, but are able to break through it, you'll discover that cognitive therapy is powerful stuff.

Researchers at the University of Pennsylvania and Vanderbilt University studied 240 depressed patients who were randomly placed in groups. Some received antidepressant medication, others participated in cognitive therapy, and still others received a placebo. After 16 weeks, the antidepressant group and the cognitive therapy group had improved at about the same rate. The real difference was that the cognitive therapy group was found less likely to relapse during the two years following therapy. Why? They had acquired the skills and behaviors to think more positively.

This example illustrates *the* key to becoming more resilient. Just like the body needs air, nutrition, and regular exercise, your mind needs a fitness regimen, too. You must regularly stretch, feed, work, coach, and rest your mind, so consider what follows as your all-access, lifetime membership to Mark's Self-Persuasion World Gym.

## The Ultimate Guide to Self-Persuasion Success

To make the most of your newfound ability to persuade in any professional situation, be sure to practice persuasion by participating in the following activities at least once a day (if not more often):

1. *Be cognitively aware of your internal dialogue.* When you make a mistake and find yourself thinking, *I always mess up!* or *Stupid! Stupid! Stupid!* hit stop. Don't keep running the video clip on a loop in your head.

2. *Reframe negative thoughts.* Don't scold. Fix. You don't *always* mess up. (You got to the office successfully, didn't you?) It's not that you'll never get anything right. (Correct me if I'm wrong, but you did land the job in the first place.) You've done many things well and you've achieved success. Otherwise you wouldn't have made it this far into the book. It's just that some aspect of a particular project or relationship is giving you a hard time. Break it down and troubleshoot. Maybe it's not the entire board presentation that's giving you fits, it's only the intro or anticipating resistance. Identify and fix. If you don't currently possess the skills to make a fix, acquire them. If you don't have the information you need, find the data.

3. *Create an honest self-assessment.* Develop a document for your eyes only. No one else will ever see it, so make a list of your strengths (how well you deal with people, perhaps, or your abil-

ity to solve problems) and your weaknesses (your dislike for conflict or disdain for details). Then add either a piece of positive evidence or a potential solution after each one. An example might look like this: "I keep my promises and am excellent at maintaining long-term relationships, as evidenced by my 10-year relationship with our firm's top client." Remember that nobody is either all right or all wrong. (Even Gandhi probably had a bad habit or two.) But with an honest assessment and a frequent review of what you do well, what you don't, and what actions you can take, you'll be on your way to destroying that pathological critic.

4. *Use success ranges.* Don't turn every situation into an all-or-nothing case. In other words, don't enter every client meeting thinking you need to come out with new business or else it wasn't a successful meeting. Create ranges of success: Your threshold success might be that you make a positive impression and set another meeting, while your ultimate success might be that you secure a deal.

5. *Understand the physical side of self-persuasion.* Get enough sleep and rest, because "fatigue makes cowards of us all." (William Shakespeare said this first, but lots of folks, from U.S. Army Gen. George S. Patton to Vince Lombardi, have picked it up, and it still rings true today.) Without enough rest, you won't be able to form your arguments, look your best, and articulate your positions to the best of your abilities. Likewise, too much caffeine hurts your persuasion attempts. Caffeine makes you seem nervous and uncertain, even if you don't have a visible case of the jitters. (So much for oozing self-confidence!)

6. *Boost your natural dopamine levels.* Exercise can fuel dopamine production in your brain, making you feel good, look good, and present your ideas with confidence. Plus, if your target doesn't say yes, it doesn't bother you as much!

7. *Be present.* Research suggests that the majority of people's thoughts are consumed with regrets of the past ("What I should have said was . . .") or focused on anxiety about the future ("What if this next guy doesn't buy?"). This makes us sacrifice the present moment, the most precious gift we have. So throw yourself into what you're doing right now, and if your thoughts start to wander, tell yourself to "get back to work."

8. *Undergo digital detox.* Turn off all your gadgets for, say, 60 minutes a day, and enjoy the quiet. Think about it: No TV. No Pandora. No Twitter or Facebook. Making digital detox a daily regimen will calm your thoughts and allow you to focus on the present.

9. *Be convinced of your own value.* Ask yourself these questions and write down your positive responses:

   - Do people compliment your work?
   - Do others ask for your advice?
   - Have you contributed an idea at work?
   - Have you sought additional education?
   - Can you produce testimonials and references?
   - Can you list best practices that you employ to be successful?
   - Have you participated in or contributed to a professional organization?
   - Do people ask for you by name?

   You might not have positive responses to every question, but you probably have more than you imagined. These accomplishments should pass through your mind whenever your pathological critic works his or her way back into your self-talk.

10. *Use positive affirmations.* In sports, team captains often can be seen rallying their teammates by yelling at them, "We got this! We got this!" While it may not be grammatically correct, from

a psychological perspective, it's dead-on. When you catch yourself slipping into negative self-talk, replace it with something positive. I realize this sounds goofy, but it works. Find a repeatable phrase and run it through your mind. I like one made famous by the late French psychotherapist Émile Coué: "Every day, in every way, I'm getting better and better." Self-help legend Brian Tracy likes to use "Back to work. Back to work." Just find one that works for you and keep using it. You got this!

11. *Create high-quality options.* When we covered persuasive processes in Chapter 7, we talked about presenting your targets with high-quality options—choices for them to decide not *if* they are going to say yes but *how* they are going to say yes. Same thing goes for you: Never allow yourself to have just one option for your persuasion project. Always have a Plan A, a Plan B, and a Plan C. Offering high-quality options for everything you do will transform your mental state.

12. *Keep a success journal.* Every night before you go to bed, write down three things you did well that day. Some people are wired to magnify setbacks in their mind and minimize successes. This isn't mentally or physically healthy. By forcing yourself to reflect on your day and capture three positive aspects, you can reverse this dynamic. Such an exercise takes incredible discipline, but if you can do this consistently, it has been said to have the same mood-improving impact as antidepressant drugs.

The psychology of self-persuasion is all about consistency. You never want to get too high when you hear yes or too low when you get a no. The tools provided in this chapter will help immensely, but it's not enough just to read this information; you must put it into practice in order for it to work effectively. Along these lines, remember this helpful rule, called the "72-hour rule," courtesy of strategic innovation consultant Aviv Shahar: If you do not use a new skill within 72 hours of learning it, the likelihood of you ever putting it to use drops precipitously.

And that brings us back to where we started this book—to the fundamental mindset for persuasion success. If you want to be convincing, you have to be convinced. The first person who needs to say yes is you.

\* \* \*

Let's circle back to that story we started at the beginning of the chapter:

The curser blinked expectantly.

*Wait a minute,* Tom thought. *This is silly. Why can't I go for that job? Sure, I don't have an Ivy League sheepskin, but I have my diploma. And more important, I have real-world experience. We've had many successes in our work group, and I've played a key role. I have a great relationship with the hiring manager's right-hand guy, and my boss has always been supportive of my efforts to improve.*

*I could pull my résumé together, run the idea of applying for the spot by my boss, and get his feedback. Any way you slice it, I have options. I can go for the job, or I could ask for some new and more challenging assignments, or I could ask to attend that immersion workshop at Penn that I've always wanted to go to.*

Tom glanced down in his hand and looked at his "stress ball" with the Red Sox logo emblazoned on it. He immediately thought about those immortal words of Curt Schilling, which many baseball pundits say inspired that 2004 Red Sox team to break the so-called Curse of the Bambino: "Why not us?"

He smiled and began putting together his application.

*Why not?*

---

## Chapter 12 Persuasion Points

1. Self-talk is good, as long as you focus on the positive and learn to overcome the negative.

2. Negative self-talk can be disastrous for your persuasion attempts.

3. Self-doubt has been hardwired into our brains since prehistoric times, so experiencing it is inevitable. The key is overcoming it.

4. Think of the psychology of self-persuasion as a "big bang theory": Self-esteem results in self-efficacy, self-efficacy breeds self-confidence, and self-confidence leads to persuasion success.

5. Know the difference between confidence and cockiness, and be sure you don't send the wrong message to your targets.

6. As psychologist Albert Bandura once said: "People with high assurance in their capabilities approach difficult tasks as challenges to be mastered rather than threats to be avoided."

7. The psychology of self-persuasion is all about consistency. You never want to get too high when you hear yes or too low when you get a no. Keep your emotions steady and intact.

8. When you catch yourself slipping into negative self-talk, replace it with a positive affirmation, as Curt Schilling did for himself and the 2004 Boston Red Sox: "Why not us?"

# BIBLIOGRAPHY

Allen, James. *As a Man Thinketh*. New York: Barse & Hopkins, 1900.

Babcock, Linda, and Sara Laschever. *Why Women Don't Ask: The High Cost of Avoiding Negotiation—and Positive Strategies for Change*. London: Piatkus, 2007.

Brennan, Bridget. *Why She Buys: The New Strategy for Reaching the World's Most Powerful Customers*. New York: Crown Business, 2009.

Brizendine, Louann. *The Female Brain*. New York: Broadway Books, 2006.

Brizendine, Louann. *The Male Brain*. New York: Broadway Books, 2010.

Cialdini, Robert. *Influence: The Psychology of Persuasion*. Rev. Ed. New York: HarperCollins, 2010 (originally published 1984).

Clance, Pauline Rose. *The Impostor Phenomenon: Overcoming the Fear That Haunts Your Success*. Atlanta, GA: Peachtree Publishers, 1985.

DeLuca, Joel. *Political Savvy: Systematic Approaches to Leadership Behind-the-Scenes*. Horsham, PA: LRP Publications, 1992.

Lobel, Thalma. *Sensation: The New Science of Physical Intelligence*. New York: Atria Books, 2014.

McKay, Matthew, and Patrick Fanning. *Self-Esteem: A Proven Program of Cognitive Techniques for Assessing, Improving, and Maintaining Your Self-Esteem*. 3d Ed. Oakland, CA: New Harbinger Publications, 2000.

Merrill, David, and Roger Reid. *Personal Styles and Effective Performance*. Radnor, PA: Chilton Book Company, 1981.

Navarro, Joe. *What Every BODY Is Saying*. New York: Collins, 2008.

Pang, Alex Soojung-Kim. *The Distraction Addiction: Getting the Information You Need and the Communication You Want, Without Enraging Your Family, Annoying Your Colleagues, and Destroying Your Soul.* New York: Little Brown, 2013.

Pink, Daniel. *To Sell Is Human: The Surprising Truth About Moving Others.* New York: Riverhead Books, 2012.

Seligman, Martin E. P. *Learned Optimism: How to Change Your Mind and Your Life.* New York: Vintage Books, 2004.

Shenk, David. *Data Smog: Surviving the Information Glut.* San Francisco: Harper Edge, 1997.

Smith, J. Walker, and Ann Clurman. *Rocking the Ages: The Yankelovich Report on Generational Marketing.* New York: HarperBusiness, 1997.

# INDEX